IT'S UP TO YOU

Second-century Gandharan stone Buddha.

It's Up to You

The Practice
of Self-Reflection
on the Buddhist Path

 Dzigar Kongtrül

Foreword by Pema Chödrön
Preface by Matthieu Ricard

SHAMBHALA
BOSTON & LONDON
2005

SHAMBHALA PUBLICATIONS, INC.
Horticultural Hall
300 Massachusetts Avenue
Boston, Massachusetts 02115
www.shambhala.com

9 8 7 6 5 4 3

Printed in the United States of America

⊗ This edition is printed on acid-free paper that meets
the American National Standards Institute z39.48 Standard.
Distributed in the United States by Random House, Inc.,
and in Canada by Random House of Canada Ltd

Library of Congress Cataloging-in-Publication Data
Kongtrul, Dzigar.
It's up to you: the practice of self-reflection on the Buddhist
path / Dzigar Kongtrul.
p. cm.
ISBN 1-59030-148-x (hardcover: alk. paper)
1. Religious life—Buddhism. 2. Buddhism—Doctrines. I. Title.
BQ4302.K67 2005
294.3'444—DC22
2004023930

THIS BOOK IS DEDICATED TO THE
ENLIGHTENMENT OF ALL
MOTHER SENTIENT BEINGS.
IT IS DEDICATED TO THE LONGEVITY
OF THE LINEAGE HOLDERS OF
ALL WISDOM TRADITIONS.
MAY THE PEACE THAT RESULTS
FROM INTELLIGENCE AND COMPASSION
PREVAIL THROUGHOUT THE WORLD.

CONTENTS

FOREWORD
BY PEMA CHÖDRÖN

I first heard Dzigar Kongtrül Rinpoche teach in the spring of 2000. I recall the talk vividly because it awakened in me something I hadn't experienced with quite the same impact since my first teacher, Chögyam Trungpa Rinpoche, died in 1987.

It was a feeling of reconnecting with a wide-open perspective on reality, as if I'd been muddling along in a small, dim room, and suddenly the walls as well as the ceiling and floor disappeared and there was a simple, straightforward freedom. I remember thinking, "Yes! This is how it always is!" I knew also that everyone could experience this and that Rinpoche was giving clear instructions on how to do it. I listened with joyful enthusiasm, feeling that Kongtrül Rinpoche was my personal link with this freedom and that I should move closer to him and learn more.

Later, after I had heard Rinpoche teach many, many times, I began to try to articulate exactly what it is in his style of presentation that resonates so profoundly. Partly, it is the prolonged and intensive Buddhist training he received from exceedingly wise and experienced masters. Somehow, both the depth of his studies and the lineage blessings of his teachers come through when he speaks. Partly, it is his life experience, which is characterized by never holding back but always challenging himself to step beyond what is secure and predictable. I find his daring and fearlessness contagious. Partly, it is his good heart, his kindness, and his humility. Partly, it is that he has immersed himself so wholeheartedly in Western culture. He knows the minds of his students with an intimacy that is possible only because he knows what it feels like to stand in their shoes. Partly, it is his almost ruthless directness. Partly, it is his humor. Partly, it's because you feel understood and appreciated. Partly, it is that you feel you can't get away with anything, that if you're hiding out or pulling back he'll address that.

Whatever the magic ingredient, I'm certainly not the only one who is supported and encouraged by Kongtrül Rinpoche's teachings. He has a great many students whose lives have been transformed by taking his words to heart and putting them into practice in their daily lives.

About a year ago, some of us asked Rinpoche to please consider taking the teachings that for several years he had been giving on Sunday mornings and making them into a book. We knew that if these talks weren't written down they could easily be lost and that if they weren't published, only the fortunate ones who had heard the talks would benefit. We wanted a far greater audience to experience what we had.

At first Rinpoche didn't seem interested, saying that he preferred to keep his audience small, hoping to see some genuine change of heart in the students who were sincerely dedicated to exploring his instructions. But as the world situation worsened, we again urged him to present the teachings more publicly, and to our delight one day out of the blue he said, "Let's do it!"

May you benefit from Rinpoche's wisdom and clarity as much as I have, and may this book serve as a personal link for you with a living teacher and the living Dharma.

PREFACE
BY MATTHIEU RICARD

Dzigar Kongtrül Rinpoche is not only a close heart-son of my root teacher, Dilgo Khyentse Rinpoche, but also one of my own teachers. So it feels as pointless and out of place for me to write this preface as it would be to strike a match in bright daylight. However, as I cannot refuse his kind and esteemed request, I will share a few words about the impact his teachings have had on so many of us.

Kongtrül Rinpoche's teachings are remarkably fresh and accessible to Westerners, but at the same time they are not a weakened adaptation of the Buddha's teachings for the West. Rather, they are an authentic expression of these teachings, formulated in words and ways that reflect his long-term experience in the Western world. Adaptations are often compromises that begin by removing the most powerful and indispensable tools of Buddhist practice. They lead us to pick up the few points of the Dharma that feel appealing and to leave out all that bothers us, like neglecting a powerful yet appropriate medicine and just applying an appeasing balm. The points that bother us are often precisely those that we need to work on because they address the deepest causes of our suffering.

For example, if the "self" really exists, to get rid of it would indeed be as painful and undesirable as removing the heart from one's chest. But if it turns out that ego-grasping is fundamentally a mistaken perception that is at the root of our suffering, what is the problem with getting rid of it? In his teachings, Kongtrül Rinpoche demonstrates with uncompromising clarity how the identification with a solid self and the resulting feeling of self-importance offer an open target for the painful arrows of anger, obsession, pride, and jealousy.

Likewise, the idea of renunciation can cast a cloud of unease upon us; surely, if renunciation means to deprive ourselves of what is truly good, it would be absurd to renounce anything. But if it simply means to give up the very causes of suffering, who would not feel great enthusiasm and adopt it as soon as possible? When a worn-out traveler finds out that half of his backpack is filled with heavy stones, isn't he delighted to take them out?

Another essential testament to the authenticity of Rinpoche's teachings is his unflinching devotion to his teachers and the strong emphasis he puts on nurturing bodhichitta, the vital altruistic attitude that leads one to realize, as the masters of the past stated, that "anything that is not meant to benefit others is simply not worth undertaking."

As someone who has been greatly inspired by the advice given in this book, I encourage you to study and practice it. Now, let Kongtrül Rinpoche's teachings speak for themselves.

AUTHOR'S PREFACE

These teachings are inspired by the needs and questions of my students as they work to integrate genuine practice with their lives. Although the teachings here are rooted in the traditional teachings I received from my teachers, I do not consider them traditional teachings as such. Rather, they are my own contemplations and insights. They are also intended to encourage students to engage in joyful and honest self-reflection as a way to deepen their understanding of the spiritual path. In the end, all teachings—traditional or informal—have one aim: to help reduce self-importance and make room for the truth.

It's Up to You is based on a series of ongoing talks that I have with my students via a weekly phone hookup. I call these talks "personal links" because they provide us with a way to keep in touch on a regular basis. They also provide a direct link to the view and the practice.

May the lineage gurus, mother dakinis, and those of great learning forgive me for any errors in this book. I urge you, the reader, to take from it whatever you find useful.

ACKNOWLEDGMENTS

My sincere gratitude to all those who have helped make this book possible. Thank you to my wife, Elizabeth, who put her heart and soul into making sure that the flow of reasoning and content was consistent with my intention. Special thanks to Helen Berliner, who put tremendous care and consideration into this project. I am grateful for her sharpness, clarity, and ability with the English language. Many thanks to Sasha Meyerowitz and Vern Mizner, who put so much time, knowledge, and thoughtfulness into the creation of this book. I am grateful to the many transcribers at Mangala Shri Bhuti for their hard work at the beginning stages of this process. And thank you to Emily Bower of Shambhala Publications for her careful attention to the manuscript during the final phases of editing. I greatly appreciate Tracy Davis's precise copyediting and John Canti's wonderful translation of the supplication.

༄༅། །ཀུན་བཟང་རྡོ་རྗེ་སེམས་དང་རྡོ་རྗེ་ཆོས། །

དགོངས་བརྒྱུད་བླ་མ་རྣམས་ཀྱི་ཞིས་པ་སྐྱོལ། །

དགའ་རབ་རྗེ་དང་འཇམ་དཔལ་གཤེས་གཉེན་དང་། །

ཤྲི་སེང་རྡྲོན་སུ་ཏ་བི་མ་ལ། །

པདྨོ་བླ་བཟང་བརྒྱུད་བླ་མའི་ཚོགས། །

བྱིན་རླབས་ཐུགས་རྗེ་ཡེ་ཤེས་རྗེས་གཟུང་མཛོད། །

མཐའ་བདག་ཡབ་སྲས་ལོ་ཆེན་བཻ་རོ་རྗེ། །

མཁའ་འགྲོའི་གཙོ་མོ་བདེ་ཆེན་རྒྱལ་མོ་དང་། །

སྐུན་བརྒྱུད་བླ་མ་སྨྲ་ཏིག་ཕྱང་བའི་ཞལ། །

ཐུགས་བརྒྱུད་དགོངས་པའི་བྱིན་རླབས་འཆར་ཕེབས་སྐྱོལ། །

སྐྱིགས་དུས་རྒྱལ་བ་གཉིས་པ་སྒྲོང་ཆེན་པ། །

འཇིགས་སྐྱིང་མཁྱེན་བརྩེ་འཇམ་མགོན་ཆོས་ཀྱི་རྗེ། །

ཀུན་སྤངས་དཔལ་སྤྲུལ་གཏེར་ཆེན་མཆོག་སྒྲིང་སོགས། །

རྩ་བརྒྱུད་བླ་མས་བྱིན་རླབས་སྤྲིང་དབུས་སྐྱོལ། །

འཇིག་རྟེན་མིག་གཅིག་མཁྱེན་བརྩེའི་ཞབས་གར་རྗེ། །

Supplication to the Longchen Nyingthik Lineage

Samantabhadra, Vajrasattva, and Vajradharma—
Teachers of the Mind Lineage, make everything
auspicious.
Garab Dorje, Mañjushrimitra,
Shri Singha, Jñanasutra, Vimalamitra,
Padmasambhava—host of teachers of the Symbol
Lineage,
Protect me with your blessings, your compassion, and
your wisdom.
Dharma king Trisong Detsen and your sons; great
translator Lord Vairotsana;
Chief of dakinis, Queen of Great Bliss,
Teachers of the Hearing Lineage, pearls in a rosary
garland,
Pour forth the blessings of your wisdom mind.
Second buddha of this age of dregs, Longchenpa;
Jigme Lingpa, Khyentse Wangpo, Dharma Lord Jamgön
Kongtrul,
Renunciant Patrül, great treasure-discoverer Chogyur
Lingpa, and the rest—
Root and lineage teachers, bestow your blessings in the
center of my heart.
Lord emanation of Khyentse, sole eye of the world;
Mighty sovereign Tenzin Gyatso, unique protector of the
world;

འཛིན་རྟེན་མགོན་གཅིག་རྒྱལ་དབང་བསྐུན་འཛིན་ཞབས། །

འཛིན་རྟེན་ཆོས་ཀྱི་གཞེས་གཉེན་འཇམ་རྡོར་སོགས། །

འཛིན་རྟེན་དཔལ་ཕུལ་བདག་གི་ལྒྲམ་རྣམས། །

ཕུགས་རྗེའི་དགོངས་ལ་ཡེ་ཤེས་སྤྲུན་གྱིས་གཟིགས། །

བདག་ནི་ཐྲོངས་ཏུ་འདུ་གསུམ་སྐུ་ཏོ་ལ། །

དམ་པའི་ཆོས་ཀྱི་སྒོ་འབྱེད་གཱ་ལ་སྲིད། །

ཉིན་ཀུང་སྤྱོན་བསགས་བསོད་ནམས་མ་དམན་པས། །

ཡེ་ཤེས་སྤྲུན་སྤྲུན་རྒྱལ་རྣམ་ཞལ་མཇལ་དང་། །

གསུང་གི་དྲིན་ཀྲག་བསྐལ་བཟང་གྱུར་པ་དང་། །

སེམས་བསྐྱེད་རྣམ་དག་བླ་མའི་བཀའ་བསྒྲུབ་ཕྱིར། །

མ་གྱུར་འགྲོ་ལ་ཕན་པའི་དག་སྐུལ་རྣམས། །

ཕྱོགས་འགྲིགས་བཀོད་པའི་གཟུགས་བརྙན་སྤྲོད་ཆུང་འདི། །

གང་གི་མཐོང་ཐོས་དྲན་རེག་གྱུར་ཚད་ཀུན། །

རྒྱལ་རྣམས་ཁྱེད་ཀྱི་གདུལ་བྱར་རིམ་གྱུར་ནས། །

དོན་གཉིས་སྤྲུན་གྲུབ་རྟོགས་ཀྲུང་ཐོབ་པར་ཤོག །

ཀྲོང་སྤྱལ་པས་མཛད་ལོ༎

Jamyang Dorje, Dharma master of the world,

And all my teachers, free from the flaws of the world:

With the compassionate embrace of your wisdom, look upon me, and think of me with kindness.

How could someone dull and confused like me, a bum who just eats, sleeps, and shits,

Introduce anyone to the sacred Dharma?

It must be that the merit I have gathered in past lives was not that small,

Since I have met in person all you buddhas with your eyes of wisdom

And had the fortune to study the meaning of what you taught;

Thus, with purest intention and in accordance with my teachers' command

Whatever I have tried to say to help my mother sentient beings,

I have made a semblance of compiling in this small volume.

May all who as much as see, hear, or think of it

Gradually become disciples of all you buddhas,

And, spontaneously accomplishing the twofold goal, attain perfect enlightenment.

Written by Dzigar Kongtrül Jigmé Namgyel.
Mangalam!

Translated by John Canti.

INTRODUCTION

The desire for happiness is universal. And beyond finding happiness and meaning in our lives, most of us want to be good, decent human beings. Wanting to be good, happy, and decent is not only a reasonable desire but also a noble one. Ironically, much of the time we struggle with how to go about accomplishing this. We have an idea of how we want to be, but we always find ourselves running up against our own doubts, fears, and insecurities.

On the spiritual path, we speak of enlightenment.* But how do we reconcile enlightenment with what we see when we look in the mirror? If we strive for enlightenment by trying to bypass our confusion, our practice will remain divorced from our immediate experience. Yet, when we focus only on our habitual tendencies, we get bogged down in our own self-absorption and pain.

This struggle to reconcile the notion we have of enlightenment with our own confusion is the very starting point of the path. It is an expression of our deep yearning for freedom and happiness, which is itself an indication of the great potential of mind we all possess. At the same time, the fact that we have this greater potential does not mean that we are completely

---

* Enlightenment is the complete and irreversible awakening to one's true nature, in which the wisdom of both seeing the true nature of phenomena and knowing phenomena in all their variety is revealed.

noble or enlightened from the start. We may have confusion. But instead of trying to either sidestep or fight against our confusion, we can make good use of it. It takes some maturity to learn to accommodate both our greater potential and our neurosis. We can develop this maturity through the practice of self-reflection.

Self-reflection is the spirit and practice of honestly looking at whatever arises in our experience, without judgment. Habitually, this is difficult for us to do; our tendency is to try to rid ourselves of unpleasant experiences and to chase after pleasant ones. The unique beauty and kindness of the practice of self-reflection is that it does not demand that we experience anything other than what we experience. Looking without bias brings both the great potential of mind and our confusion into the light of our innate intelligence. Doing so alters the historical struggle we have with our mind, transforming it into the very basis of the path of enlightenment.

Self-reflection is the common thread that runs through all traditions and lineages of Buddhist practice. It protects our practice from becoming just another enterprise by breathing life into the teachings and making them a living experience.

Part One

THE PRACTICE OF
SELF-REFLECTION

Looking in the Mirror

When we look in the mirror, the one thing we don't want to see is an ordinary human being. We would like to see someone special. Whether we are conscious of this or not, we are simply not content to see an ordinary human being with neuroses, obstacles, and problems.

We want to see a happy person, but instead we see someone who is struggling. We want to think of ourselves as compassionate, but instead we see someone who is selfish. We long to be elegant, but our arrogance makes us crass. And instead of a strong or immortal person, we see someone who is vulnerable to the four streams of birth, old age, sickness, and death. The conflict between what we see and what we want to see causes tremendous pain.

THE PAIN OF SELF-IMPORTANCE

We are imprisoned in this pain by a sense of specialness, or self-importance.* Self-importance is the underlying clinging we have to "I, I, I, me, me, me, mine, mine, mine," which colors all of our experience. If we look closely, we find a strong element of self-importance in everything we think, say, and do. "How can I feel good? What will others think? What will I gain? What will

---

* Tib. *bdag gces 'dzin.*

I lose?" These questions are all rooted in our self-importance. Even our feeling of not measuring up to who we think we should be is a form of self-importance.

We like to see ourselves as strong and in control, but we are more like a fragile eggshell that is easily broken. This makes us feel deeply vulnerable—and not in a good way. This vulnerable self requires protection, armoring, the gathering of forces, and the construction of walls. As a result, we become painfully trapped. We are increasingly fearful of relaxing with things as they are and increasingly uncertain that anything will work out the way we would like.

It takes courage to go beyond self-importance and see who we really are—but this is our path. The point of all Buddhist teachings—formal or informal—is to reduce self-importance and make room for the truth. This process begins with self-reflection.

A QUESTIONING SPIRIT

The great Indian pandita Aryadeva* once said that to merely question that things might not be as they seem can shake the very foundation of habitual clinging. This questioning spirit is the starting point for self-reflection. Could it be that this tightly knit sense of self is not what it seems? Do we really need to hold everything together, and *can* we? Is there life beyond self-importance? These kinds of questions open the door to investigating the cause of our pain.

The actual practice of self-reflection requires us to step back, examine our experience, and not succumb to the momentum of habitual mind. This allows us to look without judgment

---

* Generally thought to have lived in the second century, Aryadeva was the principal disciple of Nagarjuna, who was known for compiling and expounding the teachings on the emptiness view.

at whatever arises, and this goes directly against the grain of our self-importance.

Self-reflection is the common thread that runs through all traditions and lineages of Buddhist practice. It also takes us beyond the boundaries of formal practice. We can bring the questioning spirit of self-reflection to any situation, at any time. Self-reflection is an attitude, an approach, and a practice. In a nutshell, it is a way to make practice come alive for us personally.

OUR TRUE FACE

If we look at our habitual mind without deception or judgment, we will see beyond it to who we truly are. Beyond the "self" and what it does or doesn't want, beyond the self that is constantly fighting or tugging at the world lies our true nature and true face.

This is the face of our natural state, free from the struggle to become what we are not. It's the face of a potentially realized being whose wisdom, qualities, and courage are beyond measure. Seeing both our deeper potential *and* our hindrances, we begin to understand the cause of our suffering—and we can begin to do something about it.

When we practice self-reflection, we take liberation into our own hands. This uncompromising path demands true courage and fearlessness. Going beyond the ordinary notion of self leads directly to the truth of our buddha essence, our true face, and to freedom from suffering.

THE SPOOKINESS OF EGO-MIND

Holding to an ordinary notion of self, or ego, is the source of all our pain and confusion. The irony is that when we look for this "self" that we're cherishing and protecting, we can't even find it. The self is shifty and ungraspable. When we say "I'm old," we're referring to our body as self. When we say "my body," the self becomes the owner of the body. When we say "I'm tired," the self is equated with physical or emotional feelings. The self is our perceptions when we say "I see," and our thoughts when we say "I think." When we can't find a self within or outside of these parts, we may then conclude that the self is that which is aware of all of these things—the knower or mind.

But when we look for the mind, we can't find any shape, or color, or form. This mind that we identify as the self, which we could call ego-mind, controls everything we do. Yet it can't actually be found—which is somewhat spooky, as if a ghost were managing our home. The house seems to be empty, but all the housework has been done. The bed has been made, our shoes have been polished, the tea has been poured, and the breakfast has been cooked.

The funny thing is that we never question this. We just assume that someone or something is there. But all this time, our life has been managed by a ghost, and it's time to put a stop to it. On one hand, ego-mind has served us—but it hasn't served us well. It has lured us into the suffering of samsara and enslaved us. When ego-mind says, "Get angry," we get angry; when it says, "Get attached," we act out our attachments. When we look into the "slavish" arrangement we have with our ego-mind, we can see how it pressures us, plays tricks on us, and causes us to do things that bring undesirable consequences.

If you want to stop being the slave of a ghost, you must demand that ego-mind show its face. No true ghost will show up when it hears this! You can practice this simple meditation throughout the day. Whenever you don't know what to do with yourself, challenge your ego-mind to show its face. When you're cooking your dinner or waiting for the bus, challenge your ego-mind to show its face. Do it especially when ego-mind overwhelms you, when you feel threatened, fearful, or enslaved by it. Just straighten your posture and challenge ego-mind. Don't be gullible, wiggly, or spineless. When you challenge ego-mind, be firm but gentle, penetrating but never aggressive. Just say to your ego-mind, "Show me your face!" When no mind shows up saying, "Here I am," ego-mind will begin to lose its hold on you and your struggles will lighten up. See if this isn't true.

Of course, maybe your mind does have a face and your experience will be different. But if you don't find a mind with a face, you won't take your struggles so seriously, and all of your pain and suffering will lessen.

When we question ego-mind directly, it is exposed for what it is: the absence of everything we believe it to be. We can actually see through this seemingly solid ego-mind, or self. But what are we left with then? We are left with an open, intelligent awareness, unfettered by a self to cherish or protect. This is the primordial wisdom mind of all beings. Relaxing into this discovery is true meditation—and true meditation brings ultimate realization and freedom from suffering.

A Practitioner's Approach to Life

Looking for ego-mind is very important. This is the only way to know that it can't be found. And if we can't find ego-mind, we can't find a self—so how can we take all our thoughts, emotions, and experiences so personally?

I remember my first experience of selflessness. I felt a strong sense of freedom and a deep appreciation of how fundamentally perfect things could be if I didn't let my self-importance get in the way and complicate everything. I felt relieved to bring to light all my useless efforts to maintain a self.

People tend to appreciate nature. We associate the natural world with beauty, that which is pure and untouched. When we

see someone cutting trees or digging in the wilderness, it dis-
turbs us. We can realize the beauty of our own inner nature when
we stop manipulating everything that crosses our path as a way
to fortify a sense of self. This is a practitioner's approach to life.

If you think about it, when we grasp to a self, how can we
possibly practice self-reflection? Everything becomes personal:
our pain, *our* anger, *our* shortcomings. When we take thoughts
and emotions personally, they torture us. Looking at our
thoughts and emotions in this way is like rubbing our nose in
something unpleasant—what purpose does it serve other than
to create more pain? This is not the kind of looking we are
speaking of here.

With the view of selflessness, we can enjoy whatever arises
in our awareness. We can accept that everything that arises is a
result of our past actions, or karma, but it is not who we are.

Utilizing Thoughts and Emotions

Thoughts and emotions will always arise. The purpose of practice is not to get rid of them. We can no more put a stop to
thoughts and emotions than we can put a stop to the worldly
circumstances that seemingly turn for or against us. We can,
however, choose to welcome and work with them. On one level,
they are nothing but sensations. When we don't solidify or
judge them as good or bad, right or wrong, favorable or unfavorable, we can utilize them to progress on the path.

We utilize thoughts and emotions by watching them arise
and dissolve. As we do this, we see they are insubstantial. When
we are able to see through them, we realize they can't really bind
us, lead us astray, or distort our sense of reality. And we no
longer expect them to cease. The very expectation that thoughts
and emotions should cease is a misconception. We can free ourselves from this misconception in meditation.

In the sutras it says, "What good is manure, if not to fertilize sugar cane crops?" Similarly, we can say, "What good are thoughts and emotions—in fact all of our experiences—if not to increase our realization?" What prevents us from making good use of them are the fears and reactions that come from our self-importance. Therefore, the Buddha taught us to *let things be*. Without feeling threatened or trying to control them, just let things arise naturally and let them be.

When ego-mind becomes transparent through meditation, we have no reason to be afraid of it. This greatly reduces our suffering. We may actually develop a passion for seeing all aspects of our mind. This attitude is at the heart of the practice of self-reflection.

2

The Theater of Reflections

When we're watching a movie in the theater, we can relax and enjoy the show because we know it's an illusion. This magical display that we're watching is the result of a projector, film, light, screen, and our own perceptions coming together. In separate momentary flashes of color, shapes, and sound, they create an illusion of continuity, which we perceive as characters, scenery, movement, and language. What we call "reality" works much the same way. Our ability to know, our sense perceptions, the seeds of our past karma,* and the phenomenal world all come together to create our life's "show." All of these elements share a dynamic relationship, which keeps things moving and interesting. This is known as interdependence.

When we look around us, we can see that nothing exists in isolation, which is another way of saying that everything is interdependent. Everything depends upon an infinite number of causes and conditions to come into being, arise, and fall away moment by moment. Because they are interdependent, things don't possess a true existence of their own. For instance, how could we separate a flower from the many causes and conditions that produce it—water, soil, sun, air, seed, and so forth? Can we

---

* Karmic seeds come from the residue of past actions, whether positive or negative, and are activated by particular causes and conditions. If we have the seed or propensity to become angry, for example, when the right conditions come together, we'll find ourselves responding with aggression.

find a flower that exists independently from these causes and conditions? Everything is so intricately connected it is hard to point to where one thing starts and another ends. This is what is meant by the illusory or empty nature of phenomena.

The outer world in all its variety and our inner world of thoughts and emotions are not as they seem. All phenomena appear to exist objectively, but their true mode of existence is like a dream: apparent yet insubstantial. The experience of emptiness is not found outside the world of ordinary appearance, as many people mistakenly assume. In truth, we experience emptiness when the mind is free of grasping at appearance.

Seeing the emptiness of the phenomenal world relieves us of the heavy notion of things being solid or intrinsic. When we understand that nothing exists independently, everything that does arise seems more dreamlike and less threatening. This brings a deep sense of relaxation, and we feel less need to control our mind and circumstances. Because the nature of everything is emptiness, it is possible to view our life the way we would view a movie. We can relax and enjoy the show.

ENJOYING THE SHOW

Watching our mind can be more enjoyable than watching a Hollywood movie. The screen, projector, story, characters, and drama are all within our own experience, and all of samsara and nirvana is part of the show. Such a great theater production couldn't be bought for millions of dollars. Our ticket into this theater is "seeing through": seeing that phenomena do not exist as they appear.

Seeing through appearance—thoughts, emotions, and outer objects—is very important. When we don't see through appearance, we invest that which is fluid, changing, and ungraspable with an existence it doesn't have, and the world seems to either lure us in or threaten us. This makes peace of mind almost impossible.

For instance, something makes us angry and we just have to pursue it, get to the bottom of it, or bring it to some conclusion. We're having an intense conversation, and we just have to make our point. Or we're experiencing confusion and we have to get some clarity. One thought is just bursting to give birth to another. But at some point we need to realize that whether they are relevant or not, these are just thoughts and emotions— insubstantial and fleeting.

What if we could see through our beliefs and fears the way we see through a movie? We could begin to have fun with them, laugh at them, and let them be. Taking them too seriously defeats the purpose of everything we're trying to do on our path. We could do ourselves a big favor by just letting this discursive mind be.

From a Buddhist point of view, letting things be allows them to become what they are, instead of what we want them to be. There is a saying: "Meditation is much more pleasant when it's not fabricated; lake water is much clearer when you don't stir it up"—which means let it be. This is the meaning of self-reflection.

Not Losing Your Seat

The point of the practice of self-reflection is to experience things clearly, without muddying the waters by trying to change or control them. People who believe they can change or control everything are usually in a great deal of pain, because this is simply not possible.

Sometimes practitioners resent disturbing thoughts and emotions or feel they should be exempt from them. Those who have been practicing for many years may wonder, "Why after all this time do I still experience so much mental turmoil? Why is my mind not at peace?" This question reflects a mistaken view of the purpose of practice. No matter how advanced we may be in practice or realization, mind's natural activity does not cease. It's an expression of mind's nature, which is pregnant with possibilities. Instead of resenting mind's vitality, we can use it to deepen and enrich our practice.

The point of practice is to work with both peaceful and unpeaceful states of mind. Generally, we find unpeaceful thoughts and emotions disturbing. If they relate to our well-being, anxiety arises. But it's important to know that this is all very natural. Thoughts are the fruit of our karma; emotions and anxiety are like the juice of that fruit. Experiencing them doesn't necessarily mean you've lost your seat as a practitioner.

When disturbing thoughts and emotions arise, your only choice is to let them unfold naturally. Don't try to control or indulge them. Giving them importance only makes them more "real." Instead, shift your attitude a bit. You will see that this disturbed and anxious mind is just an expression of mind's basic nature—which is emptiness itself, and quite OK. Everything is in a good place, and there is no need for such weightiness or concern. Seeing this brings peace.

Peace comes about when the true nature of things outshines their appearance. A mind that is subtle enough to recognize the true nature of its expressions—to know that this nature is open, unobstructed, and full of potential—is at peace. For this kind of realization, we all need to practice ongoing self-reflection.

Self-reflection is the gateway to freedom. It also brings much greater appreciation and enjoyment. We begin to enjoy spending time with our own mind, and we enjoy reflecting on our experience of the teachings. Like the sun emerging from behind the clouds, the teachings of the Dharma become clear.

And the blessings of the lineage—those realized masters who have gone before us—enter our hearts and dissolve our habitual relationship with mind.

Then it becomes clear how we must use this life, and how we must relate with ordinary happiness and pain. Since both are expressions of our basic nature, striving to be happy or happier is as pointless as striving to be free from suffering and pain. In order to find peace, we must connect with our life on this very basic level.

3

The Legacy of Cavemen and Sages

From the time of the cavemen to the present, human beings have sought peace and happiness through hunting, cultivating fields, gathering material goods, and so on. We have been so busy looking for happiness and peace outside of ourselves, we've had no time to harvest them in our own mind.

Most people don't think much about the fact that greed, attachment, aggression, jealousy, and negative actions are not the causes of happiness and peace. They are the causes of sorrow and suffering. Going beyond them requires deeper reflection on the nature of mind. This basic need for self-reflection has been ignored. But without it, we have little chance of separating our intentions from the influence of others.

Society's preconditioned habits and traditions are strong within us. Yet this consensus about how to live—about what's good or bad, favorable or unfavorable for us—is simply the consensus of our conventional ancestors.* It does not necessarily imply great wisdom. Certainly there is some conventional wisdom, but most of it tells us how to create, live in, and benefit from samsara—ignoring the fact that samsara itself is a big problem.

Most of us rely on the strength of our intentions to bring us what we want. But often our intentions are unclear, or we are unable to bring our intentions and actions together for the

---

* Tib. *brda mi rgan po.* Literally, "the elders who named things."

fruition we desire. Moment to moment, thoughts and feelings arise. Every thought is based on a perception or belief, and most beliefs come from the consensus of others, whose "readings" of the phenomenal world are not all that accurate.

The consensus of conventional ancestors ignores the pitfalls of samsara and the fact that creating more samsara is a deadly trap. Its view of cultivating peace and happiness is quite ignorant: Instead of cultivating an independent sense of peace and happiness within the mind, it tries to obtain it from material sources. This consensus leads us down the wrong track.

There are many wrong tracks in society, but they are all basically the same: They all take us outside of ourselves to satisfy our inner needs. Whether they take us toward material goods or toward social relationships and emotional codependence, they all ignore mind's own potential to provide us with happiness and peace.

Unlike the cavemen, the great sages of the past sought and found independence from the preconditioned habits and traditions of society. They revolted against the great human tragedy of ignorant ego-mind and found the strength to harvest peace through looking directly at the mind. They spent their time in solitude, developing wakefulness and engaging in deep self-reflection. This unconventional path goes against the very grain of the consensus of conventional ancestors. Up to this point, most human beings have ignored the need to develop a path of wakefulness. This is the tragedy of ignorance.

There are two levels of ignorance: ignorance of the absolute, or the essential nature of phenomena, and the ignorance that prevents us from taking an accurate reading of the relative world. These two kinds of ignorance are like two kinds of thread: When they are tightly woven together, they are not easy to identify, yet they make up the fabric of delusion.

As a result of the first type of ignorance, we lack wisdom. Lacking an understanding of our true nature, we perceive that which is illusory and spacious to be solid and real. The second type of ignorance is the inability to clearly understand the laws of karma and interdependence, which then results in an inaccurate relationship to the world.

In the relative world, outer phenomena are constantly changing, our inner mind is constantly changing, and therefore our perceptions are constantly changing. We can see that everything is transitory, including ourselves. But the self, or ego, would like us to believe that everything is permanent. If we actually admitted that everything is transitory, we would have no solid ground for attachment—and ego is based on attachment.

Grasping to a nonexistent self, we misread our world and lose the true treasure of our mind. Because of our belief in a self that must be preserved at all costs, ego controls our every mental, emotional, verbal, and physical act. Although our wisdom mind is completely radiant at all times, we become like a homeless prince: a monarch who lives like a vagabond, unaware of his own inheritance.

Consequently, we ignore the way karma works. Ignoring the law of cause and effect, we forget the need to engage in actions that bring beneficial results. Instead we engage in actions that produce the karma for further suffering.

We could say that all suffering in samsara is driven by our individual ignorance and its ego. This conditioning is not ours alone; it is the predicament of every living being. The fact that the human race has survived to this point without attaining enlightenment is due to the ignorant belief in ego and its mistaken view of reality.

Without ego as our primary reference point, mind is naturally open, unconfused, and able to enjoy everything without judgment. There are many ways to describe this experience: emptiness, buddha nature, prajñaparamita, dharmakaya, or the nature of mind.* In essence, mind is unobstructed and free from ignorance, with the potential to experience everything in a fresh way. Revealing this potential is the purpose of the practice of self-reflection—and this is our natural inheritance.

---

* These terms are used interchangeably here. The nature of mind, the mind's true state, is unobstructed and free from ignorance, with the potential to experience everything in a fresh way. Buddha nature, also called buddha essence, describes the unfabricated potential for buddhahood that is present in the mind of every sentient being. Dharmakaya is the open, unobstructed, and completely clear nature of our mind. It is the ground out of which all qualities arise—both those of samsara and those of nirvana—yet it remains unaffected by either. Prajñaparamita is a Sanskrit term for the perfection of the wisdom that recognizes emptiness.

4

Our Natural Inheritance

Most of us spend our time trying to enrich our lives and make them meaningful. We strive to become influential and powerful; we work hard to become rich; or we try to achieve something meaningful through painting, music, or some other form of expression. After a lifetime of work, we may very well achieve some satisfaction. But if we had the discipline to connect with our natural inheritance, we could achieve this sense of richness and well-being in every moment.

INHERENT RICHNESS

A thick wallet and savings in the bank don't necessarily make us feel rich. Many incredibly wealthy people feel impoverished at heart. We can spend a lifetime working hard to change our material circumstances, but without inner richness, the sense of poverty and dissatisfaction never goes away. People with richness in their hearts don't depend on having the perfect outer circumstances or an abundance of material goods. They may have great appreciation for conventional riches and situations of power, but they also have a very subtle and grounded sense of richness within.

This inherent richness is called _yün_ in Tibetan. Chögyam

Trungpa Rinpoche* explains that everything depends on its own particular yün: men and women, for example, have their own yün complete within them. That inner yün magnetizes the yün of outer things. When our inner yün connects with the yün of the phenomenal world, we feel rich—much richer than most wealthy people—even with very little money in our wallet. Likewise, even with very little status or power, we feel much more powerful than many people in powerful positions. And even if we're not especially beautiful, we feel more beautiful than many people pictured on the covers of fashion magazines. How can this be?

This state of mind arises from the spaciousness and richness of our basic nature. Meditating on the nature of mind creates more space in our mind. There is more room to experience our human emotions, and more room to let the ego-mind dissolve. Within this openness we discover endless potential.

Richness and meaning don't lie outside of us. And life is not just about "what can I get?" or "what don't I have?" When we open up to the richness of experience, we are less fearful and more able to enjoy life to the fullest. We appreciate the beauty of our world and everything we encounter. With this unrestricted mind of richness, even a beggar on the street can feel like a universal monarch.

To the extent that we recognize our inner richness, we will have a tremendous sense of security that we can trust in any situation. Knowing that we can depend on ourself brings contentment and joy. Whatever arises in our life—good or bad, comfortable or uncomfortable—is enjoyable. I hope that every

---

* Chögyam Trungpa Rinpoche was a great Tibetan meditation master and teacher who planted the seeds of Tibetan Buddhism in the West. He was also a gifted poet, artist, and scholar.

one of us can at least glimpse this experience. Then we won't get so stuck in the hardships of our pick-and-choose world.

Merit and Wealth

If natural richness is inherent in all beings, why is it so difficult to experience? How can we take possession of this wealth? Is there a PIN code that we could use to access it? The answer is yes. The PIN code for richness is m-e-r-i-t. It is very important to understand how merit shapes our lives.

Merit affects everything that we are and do—and everything we will be and do in the future. Any good fortune we experience in this life is the fruit of past good actions. These are the actions that moved us toward truth and the expression of our natural goodness. We may think that our fortunate circumstances are simply due to our own hard work. But in truth, they are due to our past actions and the kindness we've received from others. Without merit, we could never experience or obtain them, no matter how hard we tried.

We all possess positive attributes—physical, intellectual, creative attributes—that make us feel special and even proud. We may possess such great wealth that we really seem to be extraordinary. But all of these attributes and positive circumstances are the result of our past actions and are not due solely to our present efforts.

If we keep this in mind, we will never become arrogant or bloated about them—nor will we feel despondent when they fade and change. If we don't identify with positive attributes and circumstances as "me" or "mine," they will never become a burden. If instead we appreciate where they come from, we can use them to shape our world through meritorious choices and actions. This is the best way to reinvest our current merit.

There are two kinds of merit. The first kind of merit clears the way for our basic intelligence and path to unfold, and in this way it brings us positive circumstances and desirable things. The second kind of merit enables us to actually experience and enjoy them.

We accumulate the first kind of merit through any action of body, speech, or mind that reduces self-importance and benefits others and through any action inspired by our longing to connect with those who have attained freedom and realized innate richness. To accumulate the first kind of merit, we use our knowledge of the cause and effect of karma to create the conditions that support the true well-being of ourselves and others.

If the first kind of merit brings us desirable circumstances, the second kind of merit allows us to actually enjoy them. Without the merit to enjoy our wealth, we are consumed by worry and stress. There is the worry and stress of obtaining wealth and then the worry and stress of increasing and protecting it. Instead of providing a sense of richness, wealth and positive circumstances have the opposite effect.

For example, you may be living in great poverty and need when suddenly you win the lottery. The first kind of merit brings you this wealth. The second kind of merit enables you to enjoy and use it well. It assures that you don't experience so much confusion, stress, and conflict as a result of your wealth that you conclude you'd be better off without it. This kind of immaturity indicates a lack of the second type of merit.

Surprisingly, this second kind of merit is more difficult to accumulate than the first. The ability to enjoy wealth comes from a deep appreciation of our world. And appreciation is only possible when we let go of self-importance. In order to enjoy our good fortune, we have to work on our mind in more subtle ways. In short, richness is our basic nature. But if we use our wealth of attributes to substantiate self-importance, we destroy our ability to enjoy them. When we let go of self-importance, we can experience the merit of appreciation.

Not appreciating our world shows a lack of the second kind of merit. We have the sun and moon and the natural world, which no amount of money can buy—but do we really appreciate them? Imagine what the world would be like if there were no mountains, forests, lakes, rivers, or seasons. Think of the beauty of each and every natural thing and how deeply it affects you.

Do you appreciate your precious human life? No amount of money could buy this human birth; you attained this life because of the first kind of merit. Not appreciating it shows a lack of the second kind of merit.

Then think of your body, and ask yourself what it would be like if you had no eyes, no ears, no nose, no tongue, or no teeth. What if the internal organs of your body didn't function well or if there were something wrong with your mental consciousness, sense perceptions, or emotions?

And do you really appreciate your work? Most of us spend our lives working very hard. If we don't appreciate what we do, we won't reap the fruit of all our time and energy, because we lack the second kind of merit. Contemplate these things to cultivate a greater appreciation for everything you have—including the lineage, the teacher, the teachings, and the practice.

Don't think that the spontaneously present wealth of the outer world—the mountains, forests, lakes, the four seasons, the twelve months, and the rotation of the sun and moon—is not due to your merit. Because of your previous positive actions, this wealth is yours to enjoy. Your human body, with its eyes, nose, ears, mouth, and so on, has also come about because of your very good karma from a past life. These are the outer and inner aspects of our human inheritance.

The secret part of this inheritance is mind. Our mind is

endowed with five incredible senses—sight, hearing, taste, and so on—that connect us with the outer world. And beyond these five senses we have the sixth consciousness, or mental consciousness. This is the ability to know and label our world. We recognize, for example, from its color, scent, and other properties that a flower is a flower. This wonderfully complex knowledge comes about in an instant, before the thought process even arises. No computer or machine can compete with this.

This sixth consciousness includes the thought process itself, which is also wonderful. It presents us with ego and the tendency to cherish and protect ourselves; it presents us with all of our negative emotions, confusion, suffering, and pain. Of course nobody wants to suffer or be in pain, but suffering does provide us with the opportunity to experience something other than a life in samsara.

Everything we experience, including suffering, arises from the essence of mind and its tremendous potential and vitality, or charge. Although we may be suffering in samsara because we're not using this potential very well, we can begin to appreciate that it's there.

Appreciation that is directed within is the source of countless good qualities. It generates openness, well-being, and humility, which provide protection from arrogance, jealousy, and self-importance. Thus it clears the way for great enjoyment of others and the world around us. The smallest act of appreciation brings great merit. It is said that offering even one prostration with deep appreciation is equal to the act of making offerings as vast as the earth to all the buddhas and bodhisattvas of the three times.

When we *don't* cultivate appreciation, we find ourselves consumed by pettiness. We might, for example, be doing a retreat in some truly beautiful place. Suddenly we realize we don't have certain things we want in our cabin, and we start sending frantically written notes to the caretaker: "I need this, I need that." Looking at this with a sense of humor, we can see how petty mind can get.

We have only one mind. If it is consumed by pettiness, its great potential is not being used in the best possible way. Not only that, we are wasting our time. Time is precious. When it's lost, there is no getting it back. With a deeper appreciation for our existence, we accumulate the second kind of merit and connect with the richness of our life.

As appreciation grows, it brings a tremendous sense of inner satisfaction. This is felt in the heart as a rich, rich feeling. If we don't feel this inner satisfaction, it shows a lack of appreciation for what we have. When mind dwells on what we don't have, we never have enough. A mind caught up in poverty mentality is missing the point.

Poverty mentality makes it harder to be rich than poor. It makes it harder to be in a position of power or respect than to have no power or respect at all. And it makes it harder to be loved than not loved at all. It is very difficult to rise to the occasion of being rich, powerful, respected, or loved because we feel split inside. On one hand, we want it all; at the same time, we feel undeserving. This gives rise to all sorts of confusion and insecurity.

THE REMEDY FOR INSECURITY

The remedy for insecurity is contentment. We all know very smart people who think very highly of themselves but who are painfully insecure inside. Their faces may be perfectly made up, but their underwear may stink—and they don't have the freedom or strength to face this. Their intelligence is devoted to impressing people so they can continue to cherish themselves.

To remedy this insecurity, we have to come back to contentment: contentment with our achievements, our spiritual path, and whatever else our good karma has given us. A sense of contentment can release all the joy that is locked up inside. To reach this place in your mind and heart, reflect not only on your natural inheritance, but also on the tyranny of habitual mind and the discontent it breeds.

To help you on this path, you have the maps left by the buddhas, bodhisattvas, teachers, and lineage masters of the past. What did they encounter on their journeys, and what did they do about it? What did or did not work for them? Due to their kindness, you have this incredible information to use and enjoy.

5

The Teacher as Mirror

Human beings need teachers. On the Buddhist path to enlightenment, the teacher shows us how to look at ourselves properly. This idea may seem simple: Look at your mind, see what you are doing with your mind, and change it. But in practice it is difficult to do. To see mind clearly, we must look without ego involvement. The teacher is especially important in this process, because the teacher points out things we can't clearly see.

The great eleventh-century Indian pandita Atisha* taught that the greatest pith instructions are those that rub hard on our sore spots. Exposing these sore spots is the teacher's job. In this sense, the teacher is the greatest mirror.

At times it may seem that the teacher is being hard on us. We may feel we're being criticized or never given a break, or our accomplishments are never appreciated. But we don't have to take it that way. Instead something wonderful and fundamental could take place: We could see those things about ourselves that we don't ordinarily see.

When I was in the presence of my teacher, Dilgo Khyentse

---

* Atisha was the master and scholar who brought to Tibet the teachings that would later become the basis of the Kadampa lineage of Tibetan Buddhism. A strict follower of the Buddhist monastic tradition, he emphasized the practice of exposing one's faults as the means of reducing self-importance.

Rinpoche,* the very evenness, clarity, and spaciousness of his mind naturally exposed my self-importance. I knew he could always see through my self-absorption, no matter how signifi- cant or complex I thought my story was. This was an unspoken understanding we had as teacher and student. This kind of communication was one of the ways I learned from him.

I saw this kind of interaction take place with others too. Sometimes people whose minds were wild—really crazy— would become immediately tamed by his presence. This is what is meant by the teacher as mirror: The teacher is the mirror that reflects not only how we are stuck but our basic sanity as well. This is the main purpose of the teacher-student relationship.

In order for the teacher to serve as a mirror, we have to be willing to look in that mirror. Otherwise we'll never find the dirt and blemishes, no matter how many mirrors we have around us. We may be afraid, but when a mirror is held up, we must be willing to look. This requires a very simple shift of mind. Even after many years of practice, it may not occur on its own. We need the teacher and the blessings of the lineage.

Our main connection to the teacher, the lineage, and the path is the fact that we are not afraid to look in the mirror. It actually intrigues us to see the various kinds of dirt and the cleaning up that needs to be done—and to know that no one can do this but us. We long to go deeper into the Dharma and truly integrate the teachings into our life. Unless the teachings penetrate us deeply, there is not much point in intellectual un- derstanding. It only increases ego. We must always ensure that the teachings are aimed at reducing self-importance.

---

* One of the most prominent Nyingma scholars and meditation masters of the twentieth century. An emanation of the great nineteenth-century nonsectarian practitioner Jamyang Khyentse Wangpo, Dilgo Khyentse Rinpoche is known for embodying all the qualities of a great practitioner. Spending over twenty years in retreat and studying with many accom- plished masters, he dedicated his life to benefiting beings. He is my root teacher.

With less self-importance and more room for truth, the blessings of the buddhas and bodhisattvas are always with us. No matter how difficult our life may be, there is nothing that cannot be changed by their blessings. In this way, in this life and the next, fruition will come—if we are willing to look in the mirror.

When we practice self-reflection in a gentle, joyful way, with great appreciation for our own wisdom as well as the wisdom of the lineage, the mind of our teacher is established within us. The teacher can feel secure about our path, because we've become self-reliant. We know that looking leads to liberation, and therefore we have the courage to practice self-reflection. Then everything we experience becomes our mirror, and every experience offers an opportunity to go beyond fixed mind.

There is no level of "seniority" where we get a break from self-reflection, not even after many practices and retreats. Such an expectation shows that we are on the wrong track. We may be tired and not wish to go any further, or we may think that we've already arrived. But the passion to look should never cease. It should deepen and increase. This is itself a sign of accomplishment.

On the path of self-reflection, you are the ultimate assessor of the beginning, middle, and end of your journey. Only you know what work needs to be done, and only you can do it. This is easy once you know how to assess yourself clearly.

Part Two

FEARLESS
SELF-REFLECTION

6

Training in Courage

Practitioners who train in courage become true warriors. The war we wage is not with enemies outside of ourselves but with the powerful forces of our own habitual tendencies and negative emotions. The greatest of these is fear. In order to become fearless, we need to experience fear. Facing fear changes our perspective and gives rise to the courage to face our neuroses as well as our enlightened qualities.

Fear and worry are understandable at times. It would be stupid not to be concerned for our personal well-being, and selfish not to be concerned for others. Feeling concern is a natural part of human goodness. But when it prevents us from accepting our life, fear is crippling. We find ourselves saying no to the world; no to our karma; no, no, no to everything—which is a very painful way to live. When we spend our life wishing it were different, it's like living someone else's life. Or, we could say, it's like living our life despite ourselves. Meanwhile, the full spectrum of our life experience goes by unnoticed.

Someone asked me recently if I am afraid to die. Truthfully, I am more afraid of not living my life fully—of living a life dedicated to cherishing and protecting myself. This fear-driven approach to life is like covering your couch in plastic so it won't get worn. It robs you of the ability to enjoy and appreciate your life.

It takes courage to accept life fully, to say yes to our life, yes to our karma, yes to our mind, emotions, and whatever else unfolds. This is the beginning of courage. Courage is the fundamental openness to face even the hardest truths. It makes room for all the pain, joy, irony, and mystery that life provides.

We especially need courage to face the four streams of human life: birth, old age, sickness, and death. A mother can't say after nine months, "I don't want to deliver my baby because I am afraid." Afraid or not, she has to go to the hospital and give birth. Mothers do this very beautifully. It's hard nowadays to find a truer sense of courage.

We cannot say, "I don't want to get old." We're getting older day by day. The way to grow old beautifully is to accept our aging and do it well. Everything is impermanent and comes to an end. Every moment that comes into being is a moment of destruction. If we accept aging as the natural process of impermanence, we will still have a sparkle in our eyes when we're old.

We cannot say, "I don't want to get sick." Sickness is an integral part of having a body. Our body is like a complex machine with many moving parts; it is subject to the suffering and impermanence of all compounded things. Think of how often you have to repair your car, which is a much simpler machine; you'll be amazed that your body functions as well as it does. If we accept this compounded body, surprisingly, we might experience illness in a very different way!

Finally, we cannot say, "I don't want to die." Everything that is born is subject to decay. We will all need tremendous courage and acceptance on our deathbed. No matter how much our loved ones care for us, we must leave them behind. Clinging to them only makes our parting more painful. We must make this journey alone. No one can experience our pain or prevent it from happening. Our death is part of our life. If we accept it with courage and joy, we will make the transition from this world to the next beautifully.

Going against the four streams of existence is like building a castle of sand by the ocean. The waves will inevitably knock it down. If we don't accept the ebb and flow of the tide, we will persist in building our castle—all the while fearing its destruction. Then we will never enjoy our life, let alone fully experience what it's like to age, fall ill, or die. But if we accept and reflect on the natural flow of aging, illness, and death, we will have nothing to fight or reject. We will not be disappointed when confronted with the inevitable—and we will have nothing to fear.

With an open mind, fear can become your greatest ally—because facing fear means facing your life, and facing your life means *living* your life. You become courageous and victorious over the world of good and bad, right and wrong, comfort and pain. This notion means a great deal to me, as my birth name, Jigmé Namgyel, means "Fearless Victory." But I think it is good advice for everyone.

7

Finding a Refuge

In the life story of the Buddha, we see that it was the realization of suffering—the suffering of birth, old age, sickness, and death—that inspired his search for liberation. In the same way, our own search for truth can be inspired by our deepest fears. It takes courage—guts, really—to look at things as they are. But if we're open to it, we may see that suffering is not what it seems to be. The willingness to look at suffering is the precursor to genuinely taking refuge.

We are all searching for a place to rest, a place where we can feel secure and at ease. And in some form or another, we are always taking refuge in *something*. The search for refuge expresses a fundamental desire for happiness. It may lead us to the Dharma—or it may lead us to unreliable refuges that leave us vulnerable to tremendous suffering.

Unreliable Refuges

Most of us look for security and solace in the phenomenal world: in our achievements, ideas, wealth, or families. The possibilities are endless. But they are all compounded, shifty, ever-changing, and a cause of suffering. For sentient beings living in the four streams of existence, suffering is all-pervasive. It doesn't take much hard thought to see that samsara is an unreliable refuge.

Many of us seek refuge in relationships. But because they

revolve around self-importance, human relations are complicated and unpredictable. No matter how highly we regard them or cherish them as a source of strength, we're always walking on eggshells. Spouses may sleep in the same bed, eat off each other's plates, exchange romantic expressions—and still not trust one another. So relationships can be thorny and fraught with dangers.

We may cherish another person, but we cherish this "I" more. It is, in fact, because of "I" that we cherish "Thee." This approach to the world is based on confusion and attachment. As long as there is a problem with "I," there will always be a problem with "Thee."

We want to forget about this part of the picture. Let's just enjoy life: Take a vacation, relax with the family, be in love. These are the reference points that keep us going. But what happens when they fall apart? It's hard to be happy-go-lucky when our world shatters while our attachments are still strong. But attachment convinces us to swallow the juice of our pain and pursue these unreliable sources of happiness.

These are the refuges we seek in samsara. They are supposed to be unfailing, but they fail all the time. They never fulfill our need for security, because looking for security outside of the mind is a natural setup for suffering and pain. Taking refuge in samsara may bring temporary happiness, but it also makes us more vulnerable and insecure—and insecurity leads to more grasping, pain, and confusion. In the end, we are left with no refuge at all. With all of our vulnerabilities and difficulties, where can we turn?

UNFAILING REFUGE

The one refuge that offers something more than an escape from suffering is the Three Jewels. With the Buddha as guide and inspiration, the Dharma as path, and the Sangha as our companions, we have a way to work with our suffering. We also have the example of those who attained liberation on this path. With this refuge, we can express our dedication to understanding not only our confusion but also our innate wisdom.

Through recognizing a true, unfailing refuge, we can see where not to seek refuge and where not to invest our trust. Without forsaking our relationships with human beings or with the richness and goodness of life, we do not turn to them for refuge. Relationships with the world are one thing; taking refuge in them is something else altogether.

Only you can know from your heart where to take refuge. Just use your intelligence to see through the concerns of this life, and you will see how well they will serve as refuges. Then turn your mind even briefly to the Three Jewels; you may find that you don't feel so vulnerable or groundless.

With a longing to take refuge in something other than ignorance and self-importance, you will discover great courage—even in the face of overwhelming disease, loss, hatred, confusion, and pain. So when you feel shaken to the depths of your being, recite the refuge prayer. When all hope is lost, simply turn your mind toward the Three Jewels. You may find that taking refuge in the Three Jewels serves you best. Seeing their power in your life will bring confidence in liberation.

REFUGE AND SELF-REFLECTION

When we stop ignoring the futility of samsara, we enter the path of liberation. Without self-reflection, we can't take this step. Habitual tendencies cause us to ignore impermanence, karma, and the suffering of samsara. We ignore the preciousness of our human birth and our potential to work with our mind. We ignore our vulnerability, which is the cause of so much suffering. When we remain in denial, even if we take refuge thousands of times, nothing will change. Denial is the first thing we must really give up.

Seeing the futility of samsara brings a sense of disenchantment, or brokenheartedness. This is the realization that everything we've ever taken refuge in, from time immemorial, has been unreliable. From this realization, feelings of tenderness and sadness* arise toward our world—along with a deep sense of renunciation. Longing to move closer to the truth, we realize there is no more genuine refuge than the Three Jewels.

This is not just Dharma "propaganda." When you take refuge, it's for your own sake. Nobody benefits but you, and nobody suffers but you when you take refuge in samsara. It is your choice: You can take refuge in samsara, or you can take refuge in waking up. But at some point, you do have to drop your doubts and make up your mind.

---

* Tib. *skyo chad*. This feeling of disenchantment or brokenheartedness is cherished by all the great masters as the root of developing genuine renunciation.

8

Dancing with Habits and Fears

From a time farther back than any of us can remember, we've habitually taken refuge in samsara in order to preserve and cherish the self. Striving to maintain the identity of who we think we are, we find ourselves driven by habits and fears. The only way to find out who we really are is to learn to dance with them.

Dancing means recognizing the raw energy of a situation and moving with it. Our usual approach is to size up situations to see if they threaten or serve us: What can I get—or get rid of? By approaching everything with a sense of suspicion and struggle, we like to think we're in control of things. But in truth our past karma is simply playing itself out. Instead of struggling with it, however, we can choose to dance.

Dancing requires us to be aware of the space and objects around us. We can't just move about any which way. And we must be alert and responsive to our partner. No one is totally in control. Learning to relax and dance reduces our fear and brings space and awareness to habitual responses. And this brings an overall sense of well-being.

KNOWING WHO WE ARE

Well-being comes, in part, from acknowledging habits and learning to dance with them. Beyond that, it comes from knowing who we really are—beyond habits and fear, beyond the worldly and even spiritual sides of our life altogether. These are all merely ornaments of our life. Ornaments mean nothing without the person wearing them. We may identify with them, but they are not who we really are. If we overemphasize their importance, there may seem to be no life or gratification beyond them. Fixating on ornaments is not a true spiritual path.

A true path is about realizing our true nature. Even lovingkindness and compassion—positive qualities to have on the spiritual path—are mere adornments of our true nature. How can we meditate on our emptiness nature when we're so busy identifying with the various qualities of our mind? Holding on tight is an egotistical trap. Instead we need to relax with emptiness, which is the open and insubstantial nature of everything. This is our true nature and true face.

HABITUATING OURSELVES TO EMPTINESS

Training in emptiness means relaxing and letting go. We experience emptiness directly by letting go of grasping and fixating on appearances as solid. These include outer appearances and inner appearances such as thoughts, emotions, and dreams. Letting go brings awareness of space. Then we can see the ornaments of space for what they are: expressions of emptiness.

Emptiness is our greatest protection from fear. We don't need to be afraid of being challenged, because there is nothing solid to challenge. We have no need to armor ourselves against destruction or cling to anything for security. Like a sky accommodating clouds, we accommodate whatever life brings—free from fear and bias. This is the ultimate mind training.

Sickness, old age, and death will come into all of our lives. But what can they actually destroy? They may destroy our physical well-being, but they can't destroy anything that is really "me." This "me" is the experience of space itself: It is open, unobstructed, and free from fear. The incredible suffering of the human realm—the pain of birth, old age, sickness, and death—cannot destroy us. When we make ourselves comfortable with emptiness, we free ourselves from fear.

By habituating ourselves to our natural state, we no longer put stock in things that, by their very nature, don't hold up. Without this understanding, life is difficult. The fears we had as toddlers stay with us throughout our adult lives. This is unnatural, but nowadays it's common. Traditionally, people had much more understanding and acceptance of life. Without this understanding and acceptance, adults are burdened with toddlers' fears. There is always something that makes our heart clench with fear of losing our well-being.

Without knowing how to dance with fears and habits—to take our place, stand properly, make our moves—we're unable to work with them. And we have to be able to work with them, because fears and habits always come back.

THE DYNAMIC OF INSECURITY

When we resist the nature of impermanence, mind is steeped in anxiety and fear. Our habitual tendencies persist in creating a semblance of security: We try to hold on to daydreams and fantasies; we try to keep fears at bay; we may even try to live a "dharmic" life. This is like rearranging the furniture while our house is on fire. Without a sense of our basic nature, we're trapped in this dynamic of insecurity.

Our modern lifestyle is permeated with insecurity and isolation. We live on the same street for years, but we don't know our neighbors. We work in the same office for years, but we know nothing about the people we work with—and don't feel we have any business asking. Although we live in the world, we suffer all the loneliness, helplessness, and other emotions of having no connection to the world at all.

At some point the people on TV seem more real than the people we live and work with. We feel we know and understand them; their scripts give us a clear idea of who they are. But there are no scripts for the people in our lives, and trying to get to know them brings up complex emotions and insecurities. At this point we feel that—other than stopping at red lights and stop signs—we really don't know how to relate to the world.

If we've been brought up in this lifestyle, it is difficult to break through our isolation and insecurity. Relationships are difficult because we're afraid of relating one-on-one with a teacher, a sangha, or anyone else. And it's difficult when situations change. Who *are* we without our morning coffee, our familiar routines and surroundings? In familiar surroundings, we don't have to face these fears. When things change, we're like domestic animals let loose in the wilderness. What will we do when things really change, when we're confronted with old age, sickness, and death?

No matter how much things change, we can always rely on our basic nature and well-being. We don't need to have so much control. We don't need to spend a lifetime holding down the same job, playing with the same buddies, and eating the same food in an effort to keep our fears at bay.

The Lively Quality of Uncertainty

Most fears arise from uncertainty. Of course, it's not very exciting to know everything in advance: It's like going to a restaurant where we've already tasted everything on the menu. But when we're stuck in fear, we can't put one foot in front of the other unless we know what lies ahead. Our life doesn't even feel like our own life, it's so controlled by fear.

If we could just let this uncertainty be, we could connect with its lively quality. Life is better when we let things be. We don't have to hole up in the familiar. We can encounter life on the level of direct experience—whatever that might be. If we don't struggle with our experience, we won't have to feel doomed or at its mercy. And we needn't feel stuck in having to achieve a peaceful, kind, or any other state of mind. We can simply be present.

As we witness our lives naturally unfolding in space, we realize that we ourselves are space. And, like a spacious garden adorned with many blossoms, all of our experiences, including habits and fears, become ornaments of this space. The basic space of unobstructed awareness is the richness we talk about from the beginning to the end of the practice path. It is *because* our nature is like space that we can function in space at all. Without space there could be no movement and no change. But thanks to space, anything is possible!

9

The Momentum of Delusion

Given that our nature is completely unobstructed, what causes the mind to struggle and spin? And what fuels its momentum?

Sentient beings are said to "spin" in the momentum of samsara's delusion. Delusion, or *trülpa* in Tibetan, is simply seeing what is not really there. The root of this misperception is ignorance. From this ongoing misinterpretation—amazingly, but painfully enough—arises a thoroughly functional world, supported by the law of cause and effect.

The engine that drives this delusion is conceptual mind, with all of its thoughts and beliefs. There is the subtle belief in a solid self that must be protected and cherished. And there are gross thoughts about good and bad, likes and dislikes, friends and foes, possibilities and impossibilities. Sometimes we engage in conceptual mind intentionally and sometimes not, but mind engages itself *all* the time. There are no breaks in its process of categorizing experience based on our preferences and beliefs.

Whether we are aware of it or not, we're caught in this unbridled momentum most of the time. Without our categories, we can't navigate our way in the world, and we certainly can't know who we are without our preferences and opinions. But in truth these concepts only ignite our emotions and undermine any chance we have for peace. Concepts and beliefs are like the wax of a candle; fueled by the wax, emotions are like the flames that keep the momentum of delusion alive.

THE POWER OF THOUGHTS AND BELIEFS

Thoughts arise continually, moment to moment; they may not even be connected. If we fixate on a thought, even a benevolent thought can become our whole world and change the course of our life. This is particularly true if we have the karmic seeds, or propensity, to go in a particular direction.

There is a Tibetan story that illustrates the power of unexamined thought very well. A man renounced his life as a farmer to live in a mountain retreat. He was so diligent in practice that he developed the power to perform miraculous feats. One day, he was given a small handful of barley seeds by a passerby. He thought, "I could eat these now, or I could plant them and harvest them later. Then I would be self-sufficient and not have to depend on anyone for food!" So that's what he did. His plan was so successful that he ended up with a whole field of barley. And he spent the rest of his days consumed by work—all because he failed to take that single thought to the path.

It is equally important to be clear about our beliefs. How do they influence our life, and do they really fulfill our intention for peace and happiness? Having strong beliefs—political, social, religious, or even altruistic beliefs—is not necessarily a problem. But when they're mixed with self-importance, we become emotionally invested in our beliefs. This leads to emotional reactions. When self-importance gets the better of us, we become self-righteous and lose the dignity of our intelligence.

At this point, we must step back and get a better perspective. How important are these views of ours? Does it help us to hold them so tightly, as if they had some intrinsic existence? Are we being disloyal to our beliefs when we have an open mind?

When you bring these subtle beliefs and emotions into awareness through self-reflection, it will be clear what you have to work on.

LOOKING AGAIN

In the West it is often said that people are driven by sex, money, and power. Now, you might think, "I'm not caught up in such things; my motivation is different. I don't really have anything to work on." But look again and you might see things differently.

I once dreamed that someone accused me of being motivated by sex, power, and money. When I woke up, I thought, "That's ridiculous! I've been working on myself for too long to possibly be caught up in such things. That person is way off base." But when I looked at this possibility honestly, I saw it was true—not in an obvious, Hollywood way, but in my own psychological way.

I could see in myself a deep longing to unite with another, which is a way of being caught up in sex. And although I've tried to avoid all the ordinary ways of getting caught up in power, on a subtle level I longed for the power to influence people and make an impact on them. This subtle attachment to power is where all gross power-craziness comes from. And when it came to money, I saw my passion for the freedom that money can buy: freedom to travel, to do retreats, to benefit others. That subtle attachment was there, even with positive intentions.

By examining our thoughts and beliefs, we uncover our deeper attachments. When they are brought to light, these concepts no longer have power over us.

SEEING THROUGH CONCEPTUAL MIND

Conceptual mind is only a problem if it's grounded in self-importance and attachment. Thoughts, in and of themselves, are illusory, fleeting, and impossible to pin down. They are neutral in the sense that they can either help or hinder us. If we understand their nature, we can use them to our advantage on the path.

Conceptual mind has tremendous power to work against the momentum of delusion and bring us closer to the truth. The study and contemplation of the Dharma, for example, can clear away ignorance. The thought of benefiting others can instantly clear away the suffering of self-importance. Used in this way, conceptual mind is a powerful, if illusory, force for counteracting the momentum of delusion.

Ultimately, however, the most powerful way to counteract delusion is to see through conceptual mind itself.

10

Slowing Down

Slowing down doesn't necessarily mean meditating. Slowing down means paying more attention to the space in your life—inside and out. It means not running off to the movie theater or becoming a zombie in front of the TV whenever you have free time. Do something more natural to slow down: Take time to rock in a rocking chair or sit in the garden and look at the lilies.

In order to slow down, we have to reconnect with the space of our life and mind. It is especially important to slow down when we're having a hard time—just when most of us have the unfortunate habit of speeding up. It's not easy to slow down and become more aware of what's going on. But in the end it will serve us well.

Some people are so speedy they seem to have caffeine for blood, even if they don't drink coffee. Being speedy is an indication of a lack of lungta, or natural energy. From the time we wake up in the morning, we're wound up in the anxiety of life's demands. We should try, over time, to slow down. With a bit more space in our lives, we wouldn't run off like robots when we wake up. We would be more present as we go through the day.

There is a saying in Tibetan that I know to be quite true: People who have a lot of lungta attend to their hair and head when they first wake up; people who have low lungta reach for their shoes. This description of someone with good lungta is really a description of someone who's not speedy. So when you wake up in the morning, sit up and feel yourself in your body. Then attend to your hair and head and go down from there. Try not to reach for your shoes first—although I always used to do this, and my mother always reminded me of this saying.

SEPARATING BASIC NATURE FROM HABIT

You may notice something very interesting when you slow down. As you experience more space in your mind, there is more distance between you and your emotional reactions. You may still react out of habit, but these reactions don't really have their hooks in you. You may react out of attachment, for example, without feeling very attached, or you may say something aggressive without really feeling the emotion of aggression. Seeing this is the beginning of being able to separate your true nature from your habits.

It's important to know that these emotional reactions are not who we really are. They come from learned social conventions, from what we've been taught to value and how we've been taught to react. For instance, someone cuts you off on the highway and you find yourself reacting aggressively, the way you've seen others do. You might even be surprised by the intensity of your reaction. In moments like this, try to slow down and reflect on your reactions. You may find them to be at odds with the way you would naturally respond.

Many habitual tendencies spring from seeds of a past we can't even trace. They lie dormant in the alaya consciousness* until they're activated by particular causes and conditions—at

---

* Known as the "storehouse consciousness," the alaya consciousness is a function of mind that stores karmic imprints of body, speech, and mind, which ripen when the necessary causes and conditions are present. It is somewhat dull and inactive compared to the more

which point we find ourselves reacting with attachment, jealousy, insecurity, or aggression. Regardless of where they come from, we must learn to disassociate ourselves from neurotic habitual tendencies. This doesn't mean not responding to things; it means bringing awareness to our reactions. Seeing that they are neither permanent nor solid, we can relate to them in a way that is intelligent and beneficial.

Emotions can only overtake us when we're unaware of them. Then it's like the tail wagging the dog. This makes us feel bad about ourselves. Tremendous self-aggression can arise in the mind that automatically reacts. But labeling our emotions as terrible or wrong has a puritanical slant. It implies that they should never occur, that we should be as pure and enlightened as a buddha. Trying to suppress reactions, however, creates explosions later. Try instead to work with your mind in a way that is more mature and more in accord with practice.

The difference between not reacting and suppressing reactions lies in awareness. The key is to maintain awareness of the *nature* of the reaction, as well as its expression. Remember that these habitual tendencies arise not just from this life. They come from many lives of reacting in habitual ways. And although they may be complex, deep, and difficult to clear up, they don't have to be so intimidating—because our habits are not who we truly are. This is the difference between nature and habit.

INCREASING CONFIDENCE

If we're not too confused or hard on ourselves, we will discover the sanity beyond habitual reactions. Identifying less with habits and more with our basic nature lightens things up. With

dynamic aspects of mind such as the sensory and mental consciousnesses, yet it serves as the foundation for all of mind's deluded tendencies. We experience the alaya directly in the first stages of sleep, right before we begin to dream.

more space in our mind, we take our reactions less seriously. We can watch them the way we would watch children at play—knowing they will quickly wear themselves out.

Seeing this happen again and again, we gain confidence. We no longer lose our sense of sanity, and we no longer become our reactions. And because we're not so concerned with the "reactor," we don't get caught in a puritanical view, or the "bad me" view of self-aggression. Even without being completely enlightened, we can see that none of this is solid or black and white. Then our emotions don't present such a danger in terms of creating negative karma—just as thoughts don't create strong karma if we don't get caught up in them. This kind of maturity is very important.

When one goes into battle, one studies the opponent. In the same way, we have to study our emotional reactions. Like all of samsara's traps, no matter how hard we try to avoid them, we fall into them. And they are more difficult to deal with than physical sensations. Physically we can work out until our muscles burn; we can put up with a headache until we can get to an aspirin. But we have very little tolerance for emotional chaos and confusion.

It is important to learn to simply relax with intense feelings such as depression, insecurity, or fear. There is no need to label them "no good" or "unpleasant" and no need to get rid of them. Just let them be. This is much simpler and more effective than trying to avoid fear or get rid of fearful things, which won't work in any case. If our mind is spacious enough to accommodate our emotions, we will discover their wakeful potential. Recognizing the incredible energy within a feeling such as fear, we become fearless in the face of fear.

Then we feel less like a dog being wagged by its tail and more like a lion or true warrior: a warrior sitting erect with the

earth solidly beneath us and heaven above. In this way we cultivate genuine confidence. Our whole being becomes very authentic, and we become much more authentic in everything we
do—regardless of our state of mind.

WORKING WITH DEPRESSION

Bringing awareness to depression works the same way. People
often feel very bad about being depressed. When we don't understand what depression is, it bears down on us. But when we
get the hang of it, so to speak, we can allow more space around
our depression and just let it be.

Depression often comes when the hidden, dark corners
we've tried to avoid actually surface. It may feel like a tight knot
in our chest or an incredible sense of anxiety. It may feel like the
earth has cracked open in front of us and we're falling into some
miserable lower realm. Or we may just feel blue.

Depression is often accompanied by strong physical sensations. In the Tibetan tradition, this physical imbalance is called
sok lung, or "wind disturbance."* But no matter what it feels like,
remember that depression is just "experience." And the experience of depression can be very valuable in coming to know all
aspects of our mind. When we come to know our mind, we feel
much freer and less fearful.

Whether depression is physical or conceptual, the important thing is to try to relax with it. Just relax with depression
without feeding it by reacting—physically, mentally, or emotionally—with fear. There is no need to fight or identify with
these habitual responses. This only makes them seem more solid
and difficult to deal with. Initially the experience of depression

---

* Tib. *srog rlung*. Literally, "wind that travels in the life-force channel." In Tibetan medical
terminology, it refers to a physical imbalance whereby the wind in the central channel is disturbed. This often causes depression, anxiety, and paranoia.

is not such a big deal; it is more like a headache. If we bring awareness to depression, it won't dominate our life.

It is important to always return to the understanding that suffering is not personal. It's an integral part of being alive and something that we all share. A great deal of understanding can come from bringing awareness to suffering, rather than thinking about or judging it. A quality of wakefulness comes with any sensation, which enables us to appreciate any experience.

BOLDNESS AND PATIENCE

The mind of practice is a poised mind. We needn't be cowardly or pushed around by any of our emotions or thoughts. We shouldn't be like the dog in a dogfight who, before any confrontation actually begins, just rolls over and gives up. When strong habits confront us, we often feel we are no match for them. But the mind of practice can accommodate the full spectrum of thoughts and emotions. We must never be intimidated by our own mind.

All of our tendencies, difficulties, and pain come from self-importance. Clinging to a self is a strong habit. We can't expect it to go away overnight. We can look at self-importance as an old bully that won't leave us alone. Dealing with it takes boldness and patience.

When I was a young boy in my village in India, there was a bully who used to pick on me. When he chased me, I always ran. One day I decided just to stand there. At first he circled me. But then he didn't know what to do. So finally he left. We can face our habits in much the same way.

Sentient beings possess varying degrees of maturity, but we all possess the same potential. From this point of view, everything is workable for all of us. We are not talking here about having great meditation experiences; we are talking about working with everyday experience within relative awareness, using our spiritual training and meditation practice as a support.

So don't think you have to leave most of your mind behind when you become a practitioner. That would be a wrong view of the spiritual path. The ground of practice is your direct experience—regardless of its content. You don't have to act out or indulge in these emotions. Just give them space and see them clearly.

11

Not Hooking the World

O ne thing that is important to face in self-reflection is the way in which we actively create pain. This pain is connected to ego's ongoing struggle to "hook" the world. Hooking is the way we try to seduce the world in order to secure our sense of self.

Getting the world on our hook is supposed to make us happy. It's supposed to make us feel good about ourselves—yet we only find ourselves creating a sticky, unwholesome relationship with the world. Right there is the cause of our pain. When we try to get the world and its inhabitants on our hook, many hopes, fears, and other complexities arise. All deep anxiety, pain, and insecurity is due to not being able to get the world on our hook or not being able to let it go.

If we want to get free of samsara, what's the point of trying to get samsara on our hook? This contradiction gives rise to all sorts of confusion and painful emotions.

DHARMA AS DARING

There always seems to be some good reason to continue hooking the world: We think it will be helpful or satisfying or good for us. When we're not busy hooking the world, we feel like a worthless person living in a lifeless desert. Whatever the reason, we feel we need something, anything, on our hook. And when we have got something on our hook, the thought of letting go makes us feel we have nothing to live for. Reasonable or not, we feel that we can't live without the world. This deep insecurity is the root of all attachment. This is the very thing we have to work with.

It is difficult to work with insecurity even when we want to, because it's difficult to let go of ego. To free ourselves from the root of attachment, we must free ourselves of attachment to a self. And our greatest fear—greater than the fear of any deadly epidemic—is the fear of losing our sense of self. But no matter how devastating it feels to let go of attachment—including attachment to a self—this is what the Dharma is all about.

As practitioners, we must question the habit of building our life on our insecurities. Maybe we should build our life on nonattachment instead. This requires daring. Without the daring of nonattachment, we can't really practice self-reflection, because we are too invested in who we want to be.

WHAT REALLY BINDS US?

In this human world, we will always need earthly things such as food, clothing, and shelter. We may live in a cave or in a large house filled with valuable objects. In either case, what determines whether or not we are bound by these things is our attachment. Without attachment, whether we have one thing or a hundred thousand things, we won't be bound by them.

The great renunciates of the Christian and Buddhist traditions, such as Jesus, the Buddha, Saint Francis of Assisi, and Milarepa,* are respected because they weren't bound by the things of this world. What made them extraordinary is not that they had few possessions but that they were free of attachment.

---

* Milarepa was a great eleventh-century yogi of Tibet, known particularly for his spontaneous songs of realization, through which he taught the Dharma to whomever he encountered. He is renowned for undertaking great difficulties in order to reach the summit of realization.

Becoming an ascetic like Milarepa or the great masters of the past is a wonderful thing. But in and of itself, it is not so important. What's important is to free ourselves of the way in which we ground ourselves in this world—and there is nothing more grounding than a sense of self. With a self to cherish and protect, we have the source of our attachment, fear, and insecurity. Then ego convinces us we need to cherish this self by hooking the world. From this ongoing effort, all samsara's suffering bubbles up like an inexhaustible spring—of which we are the source.

So when you find yourself trying to get anybody or anything on your hook, ask yourself: What am I doing? Do I really want or need this? Will it relieve my suffering and bring me deep happiness—or just complicate my life and perpetuate the habits I already have? Look, too, at the things that others think you should hook on to. You didn't come up with these ideas— to get, get, get and hook, hook, hook—on your own. The world has its own ideas about what you should hook and how you should go about it. So often we are just going along with what others want to hook for themselves, but their instincts and ideas are not necessarily good for us.

From the point of view of the Dharma, what we want most for this life is to be free from insecurity and attachment. We want to cast our earthly bonds away into nonattachment, into emptiness, into egolessness, into the true nature of all things.*

---

* Egolessness is the true state of both self and phenomena. Egolessness of self is the realization that there is not a solid, singular, permanent self found within or aside from form, feeling, perception, mental formation, and consciousness; this "self" is nothing more than a concept that we impute upon these various aggregates that constitute our experience. In this way, ego lacks even a relative existence. Egolessness of phenomena is the realization that all phenomena are interdependently originated, which means that they do not possess an independent, objective existence. They only exist in a relative way. When we realize their true mode of existence—emptiness—we realize the egolessness or selflessness of phenomena.

And when we can truly say, "I'm done with this worldly life," we will also be done with our spiritual life—because the purpose of spiritual life is to become free of worldly bonds.

At this point we can simply enjoy the unfolding of our life. With no further need to hook or reject things, we can just be. We're no longer trying to get or get rid of anything. We can witness and appreciate the karma that unfolds each day. We are finally free of the bondage of earthly things, their seeds, and everything those seeds give birth to.

We don't need to become ascetics to accomplish this. Asceticism is a means of going beyond ego attachment by practicing restraint toward material things. But even though outwardly we may have no more than a bowl to eat from, inwardly we may still have strong attachment to a self. When we accomplish nonattachment inwardly, it doesn't matter how things look from the outside. We may be hooking worldly things as a skillful means to serve some greater purpose—and appreciating everything that comes our way in the process.

Hooking the world only gets us in a great deal of trouble when it comes from basic insecurity. So when you find yourself thinking, "I need this, I want it, I can't live without it," ask yourself if this is your insecurity demanding to be fed. And if you do feed it, see if it does you any good. Does it provide any relief, happiness, or breakthroughs in your mind? If not, why complicate your life?

DESIRES BIG AND SMALL

Big desires obviously cause us a lot of pain. Wanting to become president of the United States, for example, is a big desire. But our intelligence can immediately pick up on the complications and difficulties. We will probably see that this desire is unreasonable and reject it.

Small desires, however, cause much more trouble. Subtle desires arise every day, every hour, every moment—and we do not usually think them through. We may not even see them. If we do see them, we may disregard them as small and reasonable: What's wrong with having that cup of coffee or chocolate bar—even if it's bad for me or makes me crazy? These small desires take up much more mental space than big desires and create much more suffering.

We can see, for example, that a "big" desire to have a relationship with a Hollywood movie star is unreasonable. As much as we would like to enjoy this beautiful person the way we enjoy him or her in the movies, we probably won't pursue it. But what about the person who is conveniently within reach? That person might be easy to get into our web. These small earthbound desires are the ones that get us. They spring from dormant seeds of self-clinging and keep us stuck in samsara.

One way to lessen out-of-control desires is to appreciate what we have. Then we don't need to chase after petty things and get caught in petty ego-mind. And we won't make the mistake of thinking that our small desires don't have big or painful consequences. The pain is there even as we indulge in them— and the end result is staying stuck in the cycle of samsara's suffering. If we understood the mess we would wind up with in the end, we would never cling to the self with all its attachments and desires. We would be much more aware and not so naïve, and we would do whatever we could to be free of it.

IMAGINING THE UNIMAGINABLE

Any long-held habit is difficult to let go of, and we've been holding on to a self longer than anything else. The thought of letting go generally creates fear and insecurity. It's like banging your head with a hammer for aeons, then being afraid to stop because you can't imagine what relief would be like. Habits create that kind of fear. As scary as it is to think of letting go of attachment to family, friends, and possessions, it's not nearly as scary as letting go of everything—ideological and practical—that we cherish as a self.

It is very difficult to imagine not having a self. It would be like not having a house to come home to. We can't conceive of living life without that kind of security.

The unimaginable strikes fear in our heart and creates endless insecurity. Then the hooking of the world begins—spiritual hooking, worldly hooking, the hooking of things we don't need but feel we must have—and our lives become very complicated, cluttered, and dependent on outside things. Instead of helping us to live life fully, our "house" actually binds us. Without it we could move about freely and easily.

Maybe it's not so important to have this house. Maybe we could let go of everything and live in the fresh air. This kind of confidence is very daring, very challenging, and very liberating.

MEDITATION ON EGOLESSNESS

Meditation on egolessness is called "the meditation that leads beyond the cycle of samsara." In meditation we train to go beyond the ordinary passions of ego. If our meditation is not free from these passions, it is very fishy—no matter how good it seems to be. Being aware of fishiness is a good safeguard for our meditation. Without awareness, even small thoughts—"I think I've got it, my meditation feels right, this makes me feel good"—can contain a big sense of self. These thoughts themselves are not the problem. What makes our meditation fishy is the cherishing of ego and the failure to remedy ego's tendencies.

My wife, Elizabeth, noted an irony: When we practice, ego doesn't help us at all, but when we have any kind of achievement, ego takes all the credit. If we let this happen, we are letting ego destroy us in the end as well as in the beginning. In the beginning, ego creates obstacles. In the end, it can destroy our accomplishment by taking credit for it.

When practice becomes a possession for the ego, we may find ourselves asking: What is the point of meditating to become free from ego? How will we enjoy anything if there's no enjoyer? And what if meditation deflates our passion? That would be devastating. We like to keep our passion balloon filled. Letting the air out would cause us to lose heart. Our heart is so pumped-up with ordinary passions that any encouragement to let go feels like a puncture. We suspect that egolessness might lead to a sense of depression, carelessness, or complete loss of interest. If there's no reason to do anything, we might as well just crumple up!

This is a misunderstanding of egolessness. Attaining egolessness does not mean we crumple up, disappear, or lose our "juice." Nor do we isolate ourselves from the world and its apparent richness. Egolessness simply means letting go of grasping and fixation, hopes and fears, and the tendency to hook the world.

Only a mind that has not reflected deeply on the suffering of samsara could believe that happiness is obtained through ego's ordinary passions. The mind of egolessness, on the other hand, is wiser. It knows the cause of suffering and can discriminate true pleasure from pain. Therefore, it has tremendous passion—passion to go beyond the limitations of samsara. Beyond ordinary passion, there is a passionless state of unconditional joy and contentment.

A heart filled with egolessness experiences life to the fullest. So when you're passionately trying to hook the world, take a look at what you are doing. Does it really serve you—or is it just another hook into suffering? Then ask yourself who is doing the hooking. In some sense, we are all "hookers." If you don't want to get stuck in the hooker syndrome, follow the path of egolessness.

12

Being Present

Most of us have had the experience of sitting by the seashore or on a mountaintop, simply enjoying the beauty of nature, relaxed, content, and present. We've probably also had the experience of sitting by the seashore or on a mountaintop and missing it completely. Being present—or not—is a basic human experience.

Sometimes when I'm stuck in traffic, I look around at the people in the other cars. Here we are, all stuck in the same traffic jam, but all in our own separate worlds. And I can see just by looking at people's faces that these worlds are as different as Earth from Mars. We are isolated from our lives whenever we are living in our own bubble of restlessness, distraction, or self-absorption. This isolation is fueled by the hopes, fears, and fantasies that prevent us from being present and experiencing things directly.

Being present doesn't mean being in a blank or thoughtless state. It means not needing to escape from where we are. Being present brings contentment. We don't need to look for a better thought, a better emotion, or a better place to be. When we operate from ignorance—when we're daydreaming, carried away by thoughts, and unaware of our true nature—we have no presence of mind. We don't even know such a state exists.

Thoughts don't necessarily prevent us from being present. There is no controlling their comings and goings, in any case.

We just need to be able to see through them. The best example of this is when you are asleep and you recognize you're dreaming. The flow of the dream doesn't change. You are still aware of the dream's imagery and content. But there's some distance from it: You know you're dreaming and you are present with your dream.

Most of the time we simply don't want to be present—because what would we do then? How would we pursue our goals or become the person we want to be? Confusion enters our mind and, instead of being present, we would rather be some different person in some different place.

BEING DIFFERENT

If we look back on our lives, most of us can remember always wanting to be different than we are. Although we may have been quite present as an infant suckling our mother's milk, even as a young child, we wanted to be different—bigger, more powerful, more grown-up. Or maybe we just wanted to be a different child, a stronger or more attractive child with better clothes and toys.

Craving what we don't have and wanting to be what we're not is a basic human condition. We all want to move forward and obtain all the things we can get out of life. Especially in the United States, people feel that the pursuit of happiness and success is a birthright. But because we can't hold both craving and contentment in our awareness at the same time, craving keeps us from appreciating who we are, where we are, and what we have.

When craving is fueled by ambition, we may feel we deserve things that are beyond our karma to acquire. Believing that we are entitled to whatever we want shows a lack of respect for the cause and effect of karma. It shows a lack of understanding of the impact of the deeds of our past lives, and no understanding of merit.

SEEING THE WORLD AS OUR TANGERINE

Our parents and environment may convince us that we're very special: Just look at our intelligence, sharpness, and beauty. As the product of our parents' seed and egg, we're the crème de la crème and we deserve the best. We get caught in this idea from a very young age.

In school, any comparison with others is usually competitive. We are not taught how to reflect upon ourselves clearly, without judgment. Nor are we taught to assess our character in light of others' qualities in a noncompetitive way. As time goes by, ego only develops further—along with the feeling that we're extremely special and talented. If the world only knew who we were, it would bow down at our feet.

On a subconscious level, however, there is a constant feeling of discontent, which is caused by craving and fueled by ambition. This discontent distorts the way we look at the world. We see only what we can get instead of what we can give. We see the world as our tangerine, and we are always looking for ways to squeeze out more juice. There is no sense of a dignified human commitment to the world. There is no sense of wanting to contribute to the larger human community of which we are a part. If these negative tendencies of craving and egotistical ambition continue unchecked, we will never be content or happy with who we are.

Now, the Buddha never said these tendencies were negative by definition. They are negative by virtue of our experience. We have seen clearly that they cause problems and suffering. Since childhood we've been tormented by a state of mind that nothing has really changed. We still look for safety and security outside of ourselves. And our main concern is with what we do or don't have and with the people we want in or out of our life. This is the motivation of greed, attachment, and denial of impermanence and suffering.

We may have even entered the spiritual path. But nothing will change inwardly unless we challenge the tendency to cherish and protect ego. Outwardly, we may seem to be a more spiritual person intent on a genuine spiritual path. But if we want our path to feel safe and secure, everything will stay the same. The Buddha taught us to reflect upon these tendencies.

THE CHALLENGE OF SELF-REFLECTION

Without self-reflection, what would a spiritual path be, and where would it lead us? We might simply become pacifists, trying to change the world or fit into some community or social group—but still confused about who we are as individuals and why we're pursuing a spiritual path. There would always be a dichotomy between our spiritual path and the way we live our lives, and so nothing would change. We'd be like a train with its wheels on two tracks, trying to go in two different directions at once.

In some sense every path, conventional or spiritual, is about the pursuit of happiness and liberation from suffering. With the Dharma, the teacher, and the practice of self-reflection, we could begin achieving these goals here and now. We could do this by going beyond the habitual tendencies that cause suffering and pain. But are we really willing to change our approach? Are we willing to be present long enough to see our habits? This is the challenge of self-reflection.

The possibility of change exposes our love affair with ourselves. And no matter how painful that relationship has been, we may suddenly question our willingness to change. Most of us like ourselves very much. We are somewhat addicted to being who we think we are. Maybe we could just keep it that way. The idea of change feels like being unfaithful to ourselves. So we resist change and become illogically stubborn about holding on to habitual patterns.

Resisting Change

We love our strategies and goals and our cunning way of looking at the world—as a ripe tangerine just waiting to be squeezed. We love the drive and speed with which we get things done, even though we may not enjoy doing them. We even love all the negative emotions—anger, jealousy, attachment—and the complex levels of our pain. If we get rid of them, will we still be a human being, or just a lifeless piece of wood? The buddhas and bodhisattvas, of course, are not pieces of wood devoid of emotions. But because we're afraid of losing our spark, we resist change.

We want to be who we want to be, which is who we've always been. We are reluctant to look inward and see our pain—even after taking refuge in the Three Jewels, even after so many opportunities to hear, reflect on, and practice the teachings. Even during practice or in retreat, with all the advantages of a good place and good support, we may still resist transformation.

If this stubbornness continues, the Dharma might become a social identity and practice might become a social activity—but the work of the path will not get done. Nothing will change in terms of our being an ignorant human being cherishing and protecting a self, with all the habitual tendencies, discontent, and cravings that make life so miserable. The amount of confusion and neurosis stewing in our life won't change at all. Given all this, not wanting to change could be seen as an illogical and stubborn attitude.

Seeing the stubbornness of sentient beings causes the buddhas and bodhisattvas great pain. If they have any pain at all, it is this. And there is nothing they can do until we are inspired to change our approach. This inspiration must come from within us. This is why it is sometimes easier to "wake up" when we're in extreme pain—not just the pain of our habitual stubbornness.

BEING PRESENT WITH APPRECIATION

When we are present and awake, habitual tendencies arise but they also dissolve. From time to time, we may get caught and spin off. But as soon as we realize it, our presence of mind brings us back. When we are present, we experience so much greatness and achievement within, we might wonder why we ever try to achieve fulfillment outwardly. At this point, we begin to truly appreciate our life and our world.

Appreciating your world comes from being present in the world with a sense of wonder. The world is so beautiful. No artist could create the beauty of the natural world with its sun and moon, rivers, forests, meadows, animals, and four seasons. It is all spontaneously present for your enjoyment. If you're present, you can appreciate how the sun's rays warm your body and how each snowflake falls. The great fourteenth-century scholar and lineage master Künkhyen Longchenpa* described his experience of a breeze as the enjoyment of feeling all the hairs in the pores of his skin moving in the wind. When you can appreciate each hair in each pore of your skin moving in the wind, you won't need any other world.

Appreciating your body—fat or thin, pleasing or not—is

---

* Künkhyen Longchenpa was the most famous and important scholar–meditation master of the Nyingma school of Tibetan Buddhism. He was responsible for compiling, expounding upon, and writing commentaries on the vast literature of the Great Perfection, thus preserving these teachings, which have become widespread.

also important. The body grounds our consciousness in this world. It is said that after death, the mind in the bardo* is seven times speedier than the mind of a schizophrenic. This is because we no longer have the ground of a physical body. Now, some of us may be speedy, but not like that. So no matter what kind of body you have, you should appreciate it.

The body's whole system of sensory organs enables you to see, hear, smell, taste, and feel the world. Just look at the vegetables in your kitchen. You couldn't use them as food if you didn't have a body. Your body makes it possible to chop them up, spice them, cook them, and make them into a delicious dish to eat. Then the body actually digests them and nourishes itself. A being without a body, a bardo being, for example, could only look at the vegetables as if they were a painting. But there would be no connection with them—no eating, digesting, or nurturing. As long as your body lasts, you can enjoy this world. So no matter what kind of body you have, enjoy it. Wanting it to be different creates body-image problems. Your body is wonderful just as it is.

Appreciating your mind reveals such a great gift of nature. The ability to perceive the world at all is a gift of the mind. Have you ever contemplated what it would be like to have no eye consciousness and not be able to see? Or to have no hearing, smell, or taste consciousness? And without the mental-consciousness, or awareness, to know what you perceive, you wouldn't be able to understand, remember, or reflect upon things, basic or sublime. When you are truly present, you can appreciate your mind and its many functions.

The human mind's greatest potential is the ability to wake

* Tib. *bar do*. The bardo is the state between death and rebirth. More subtly, bardo refers to any transitional period between one moment and the next.

up, to free itself from ignorance and benefit beings. No one had to give you this ability; it is yours by virtue of your precious human birth—and the willingness to be present. You don't need much more than this, inside or out. Outwardly, all we really need to sustain life is food, clothing, and shelter, and it's said that any practitioner who takes refuge in the Three Jewels will obtain these for sure. Even if you hide yourself in a cave like Milarepa, you will be certain to get these three things. So you shouldn't have any concern about that—and beyond that nothing is necessary.

Appreciating the Dharma provides your greater purpose in life. To achieve this requires patience: patience to practice, study, and focus—and to *not* be stubborn and unable to change. With patience, the teachings and practices open up to you naturally. Patience enables you to be present and awake for this. Then the world opens up magnificently for your enjoyment.

We don't have to travel from this world to some better world to enjoy greatness. When we simply wake up, our relationship with this world changes. Day to day, month to month, year to year—the world becomes more magical and unimaginably beautiful. Something we saw five years ago will appear completely different to us after five years of awakening. At this point, our life and everything in it becomes a source of immeasurable appreciation. It is impossible to really describe this sense of joy and contentment. Nevertheless, we must try to understand it and discover it in our own life.

When the true nature of things is revealed, there is no confusion, no samsara, and no sentient beings suffering in samsara. Everything around us has the potential to transform this life. So we really have great reason to be present—and not caught in the momentum of craving and discontent.

13

Going Beyond Self-Importance

It is not easy to contemplate being held captive by anyone or anything—let alone ego! We may feel panic and resistance at the very suggestion. But we are even now being held captive in samsara by our largely unconscious sense of self-importance. Without keen awareness of our self-importance, we can't free ourselves, because self-importance shapes our relationship with the world, the spiritual path, and our mind.

Even with great diligence in practice, and with practice experiences as many and varied as wildflowers in the spring, all of our accomplishments will belong to ego if the ground of our practice is the desire to be special. We may think that we're great practitioners making progress on the path, but actually our self-importance may be getting more solid.

As our mind becomes less pliable, we become more isolated from our teacher and the wisdom of the Dharma. If we don't get the recognition we feel we deserve, we may lose our appreciation for the teacher altogether. The spiritual path becomes a disappointment. And nothing seems to be working in our favor— particularly on the path of liberation from self-importance.

If we are unwilling to work with ourselves, we may come to believe that we don't need anyone—no lineage, no Three Jewels, no teacher, no friends. Lacking the confidence to let go of control, we try to fix all of our problems on our own. With such an attitude, no one can get close enough to truly see us, and we

certainly don't want to hear anyone suggest that we may have
some faults, even if it's true. Such suggestions might shake the
foundation of our identity and rattle our world. We might have
to relearn everything from A to Z! From this sense of uncertainty, we reject the whole thing.

But even if the world were to honor us with everything it
had, if people offered us their hearts and lives, it still wouldn't be
enough to ease our pain inside. Why is this? It's because self-
importance has no interest in how ego works. It has no interest
in looking in the mirror and seeing its true face.

Even when self-importance doesn't manifest as arrogance
or pride, when it has the look of total humility and selflessness,
it still has no real interest in self-reflection. So we continue to
operate in the habitual ways that cause us tremendous pain. We
may feel some renunciation toward the pain; even animals and
newborn children feel renunciation toward pain. What we
need, however, is renunciation toward the cause of pain, which
is self-importance.

THE SPIRIT OF SELF-REFLECTION

Through deep self-reflection, we see that less self-importance
means more room for the truth. Understanding this brings
tremendous appreciation for the lineage masters and a longing
to follow their example. How did they manage to let go of the
attachments that surge up from mind's habitual tendencies?
They did it by seeing their own faults, by seeing their own de-
ceit and cunning and all of their worldly attachments. By ultimately letting go of attachment to a self, they abandoned the
cause of suffering and realized the simplicity of self-existing
buddha nature.

Their example shows us the benefit, joy, and real spirit of
self-reflection—which is an actual passion for exposing our

hidden corners and faults. It shows us that *looking* leads to liberation. So when someone says that we're arrogant—or a miserable, lowlife, ego-scheming, greedy, pathetic person—we can appreciate that. We can't always see these things on our own, but the truth within us recognizes them when they're exposed. We should feel grateful to anyone who has such insight or connection with us, because this is our real work.

Whenever someone points out your real work, try to appreciate the benefit of that. You don't have to armor yourself or rally your self-importance. Harboring such insecurity is like harboring a terrorist in your mind: No matter how beautiful and supportive your world is, ego is terrorizing you all the time. And it will continue to terrorize you until you get to the root of the problem, which is self-importance. So don't be afraid to look in the mirror and see yourself clearly. Even your arrogance and sense of specialness are just ordinary suffering and pain.

Seeing the World as Our Teacher

Any feedback that assaults our ego is a blessing in disguise. If we're willing to see the world as our teacher, we appreciate the honesty. We are not afraid to be blamed, cut down, shredded, or destroyed or to have our feelings hurt. Decent people do not subject themselves to this kind of abuse, but in this case we appreciate it—not because we're masochistic but because of the greater vision we hold inside.

Of course, most of us prefer to rely on the honesty of our friends and those we trust. But great practitioners such as Patrül Rinpoche, Shantideva, and the great mahasiddhas of the past* didn't care where it came from. They were only concerned with seeing through their own faults and self-importance.

* Mahasiddhas are accomplished or enlightened beings, particularly those who adopt unconventional forms and methods in order to awaken students and "shock" them out of their

The ability to take feedback from the world—with or without a personal relationship or connection of trust—depends on our strength and focus as a practitioner. The more we welcome feedback regardless of its source, the deeper we will go in our practice. No matter how it comes to us, the phenomenal world is our teacher. And the teacher will help us do our real work, even if it hurts.

From this point of view, we *want* to open our can of worms and look at them more closely. We want to free ourselves from all of ego's attachments, not just some. No matter how deep the pain, challenge, or panic, we welcome it. No matter how shaken our solid world becomes, we appreciate it—and we deepen that appreciation until it becomes indestructible. We realize that the only real threat to our well-being is self-importance. This is what we need to renounce.

RENOUNCING SELF-IMPORTANCE

Renunciation arises in the mind with the taste of suffering and pain. But even when we taste suffering for ourselves, we may still prefer to hold on to our small world rather than face the unknown. Without great faith in something other than ego, it's frightening to face the unknown. We may not want to admit it, but we prefer to stay stuck. We may think if we volunteer our services to ego—even if it means acting foolishly and mindlessly—we might feel more "secure."

This is the ultimate form of brainwashing. Many people are

---

ignorant delusion. Patrül Rinpoche was a great nineteenth-century Tibetan master known for his extremely simple wandering lifestyle, humble demeanor, and exceedingly profound teachings. Among his many famous and enduring texts, *The Words of My Perfect Teacher (Kunzang Lamai Zhalung)* is one of the most widely read books among Tibetan practitioners. Shantideva was an eighth-century Indian master renowned for his spontaneous composition of *The Bodhisattva's Way of Life (Bodhisattvacharyavatara)*, one of the most important and widely studied texts of the Mahayana tradition.

afraid of being brainwashed by religion. But there is no fear of brainwashing in Buddhism; we know we are already brainwashed by ego. Because ego does nothing but create pain and suffering, Buddhism is about getting unbrainwashed. It's about waking up from this hypnotic state of subservience to ego. Through meditation and self-reflection, our own awareness bears witness to ego's "indoctrination." We begin to see the significance of the Buddha's journey and teachings, and we see the significance of the sangha, the lineage, and their blessings.

It comes down to this: By renouncing ego's sense of specialness, we renounce all the ways that ego lays claim to us. If we don't renounce specialness, all of our life decisions will be made by ego. Ego will be our guide on our path—in which case our path won't go anywhere.

Humility is essential to this process. We are all ordinary human beings working with ordinary problems. It helps to always see yourself as a beginner: as a child crawling about, or sucking its mother's milk, or just being born from the womb. You are incredibly vulnerable, but you have tremendous potential to go beyond all ignorance and suffering. With humility, you will never become full of yourself. You will always have the openness to look—and through looking, to renounce self-importance and assure your well-being.

14

Distinguishing Friend from Foe

If we want to go beyond self-importance, we need to undermine ego's logic. Ego's logic is always based on self-cherish-
ing; ego leads us to believe that we will find happiness through
putting ourselves first. Yet, try as we may, we have never been
able to succeed in living a life of contentment through catering
to this ego of ours. It never makes us happy enough, rich
enough, beautiful enough, or secure enough. Although ego
would have us believe otherwise, focusing solely on ourselves
does not bring happiness. In truth, on the path to freedom and
happiness, self-importance is our greatest foe.

This foe—so self-concerned and controlled—has one
great vulnerability. It is vulnerable to the powerful forces of
loving-kindness, care, and compassion: when we extend the
very care we have for ourselves to others, it frees us from our
self-importance and brings true happiness. Making others the
focus of our care reverses ego's logic. You can see for yourself
how this frees up your mind.

Although we are habituated to putting ourselves before
others—and tend to think small—in the long run, we live in
this world and we are deeply connected to others. When we
give something to the people around us, the world is beautified.
When we help others and extend to them, their conditions
improve. They appreciate this and we find that our own lives

become better. Cultivating an altruistic mind that cares for others is a powerful approach to overcoming self-importance.

We habitually think it is better to gain than lose. But if we are happy to lose for the sake of others' gain—if their happiness becomes our happiness—we will always be happy.

In this way, other beings become the cause that liberates us from our self-importance. This is why we say that all living beings are our greatest friends.

Without knowing who is friend and who is foe, how can we make clear decisions about our path and our relationship to others? Learning to distinguish friend from foe creates a revolution in the mind of a practitioner. A practitioner is someone who has been transformed from the inside out. The "revolution" that a practitioner experiences transforms negative states of mind into clear, positive patterns of thinking. This transformation is based on direct experience, not delusion. It is not just intellectual; it's not just a change of mind. The heart is deeply transformed as well. The definition of a true practitioner is a person who has developed an awakened mind together with an awakened heart.

15

Stretching the Heart Further

There is joy and happiness in samsara, but it doesn't last very long. Happiness goes by in the blink of an eye, and pleasure is followed by pain and suffering. In the modern world, we expect to be comfortable and in a good state of mind all the time. When we're troubled, we wonder what went wrong. In fact, we simply live in an unreliable world—and there is no escaping it.

SUFFERING IS UNIVERSAL

There is no escape from birth, old age, sickness, and death. We're not doing anything wrong when we feel troubled; we are simply not accepting our karma. How can this unreliable world provide us with lasting happiness? And how could we possibly feel compassion if we don't accept samsara and the suffering it brings to all living beings?

Suffering is a universal experience. All living beings are subject to ignorance, karma, and pain. Instead of turning away from this or seeing it as useless, tormenting, or destructive, we can use this pain to develop compassion.

Of course, if we felt only *our* pain and not the pain of others, we would be self-absorbed. If we saw only *their* pain without recognizing our own, our compassion would remain abstract. And if we saw both our own *and* others' pain without understanding that suffering is the nature of samsara, we might simply conclude: Life is suffering and the best we can do is help each other get through it. But there is no vision in this approach. Instead, seeing that the nature of samsara is suffering, we must look to the cause.

IGNORANCE IS IMPERSONAL

The root cause of suffering is ignorance. Ignorance is the ground of all actions and experiences in samsara. In the sense that it is universal, we can say that ignorance is impersonal. We're all equally subject to the karma and suffering arising from ignorance. In this respect, we are all innocents, really. We don't need to blame ourselves—or anyone else—for our suffering. Instead we can blame ignorance.

Nevertheless, ignorance does create karma, karma does ripen in all beings, and all beings do suffer. This poignant truth generates compassion for ourselves and all living beings.

Compassion changes our mental attitude and emotions. We immediately lose our self-pity and self-absorption. We no longer indulge in denial of suffering, and we are no longer desperate to feel better—which is a pain in itself. Instead we can use suffering in a meaningful way to wake ourselves up. We can use it to develop a limitless heart of compassion and a strong feeling of connection to others. This reduces our sense of specialness altogether. When, like the buddhas and bodhisattvas of the past, we wake up deeply from ignorance and delusion, we can live a life of compassion and service to others.

THE LIMITLESS HEART

It's a big stretch for the heart to go from having room for one person—or the few people close to us—to having room for all living beings. We will feel some pain. The heart, however, is elastic. If we challenge it to grow, the heart can stretch to the limits of space without breaking. In the same way, our intelligence, which is so limited when we think only of ourselves, has the wisdom potential to aspire for the enlightenment of all beings.

Having enlightened potential doesn't mean we're about to explode; it means we have the power to grow. We should be grateful to anything that challenges our heart to stretch and go beyond small-mindedness—because what is the point of a life devoted solely to self-preservation?

When we're born, the placenta wrapped around us for survival in the womb is ripped away so we can breathe. Recreating a womb of self-importance is like never having been born at all. If we're only concerned with our own comfort and protection, there is no sense of courage. We can stretch beyond these limitations by replacing self-concern with concern for all sentient beings.

According to the Buddhist view of rebirth, it is said that all sentient beings have, at one time or another, been our mothers. Contemplating their great kindness and protection gives rise to feelings of great kindness toward all sentient beings. And when our heart feels hard and small, we can soften our heart by remembering this kindness.

This is the ultimate challenge for a practitioner: the great and deep practice of bodhichitta.* The bodhichitta teachings of awakened mind and heart encourage us to see that all living beings have the same wish for happiness and freedom from pain. They inspire us to bring all mother sentient beings out of suffering to true happiness.

---

* Literally, "enlightened heart." On the relative level, bodhichitta has two aspects: aspiration bodhichitta, which is the wish to attain enlightenment for the benefit of all sentient beings; and engaged bodhichitta, which includes the practices of the six paramitas. Absolute bodhichitta is insight into the nature of all phenomena.

THE KINDNESS OF OUR MOTHERS

As newborn babies we are vulnerable and helpless. We can't even wipe away our own tears. But through our mother's kindness and protection, we are able to grow to adulthood and reach some of our potential. Due to our kind mother, we can feel the warmth of the sun on our skin and the coolness of a breeze. Because of this human body given to us by our kind parents, we have the opportunity to practice the Dharma and engage in benefiting others.

If we really understood the boundless kindness and care that mothers extend to their children, we would feel a sense of burden and sadness in our heart—and a sense of profound appreciation. Appreciation fills our heart with warmth and joy. To repay their kindness, we want to extend this warmth and joy to all mother sentient beings suffering in samsara.

No being can bear suffering; even animals constantly strive to free themselves from suffering. Unfortunately, not knowing the causes and conditions that lead to happiness, they continue to suffer incessantly. Sentient beings are like a blind man in the middle of a busy intersection: so confused and vulnerable! Helpless to get where he wants to go, he can only stand there afraid to take even one step. This is the predicament of all mother sentient beings living in samsara.

In a big city like New York, we can see so many human beings rushing in and out of the subways and along the street. And what are they doing? They are all pursuing happiness, in one form or another. Flying over cities like Los Angeles, Calcutta, or Beijing, we can imagine the people living in all those tiny houses below: a family, a couple without children, a bachelor, an old woman, a student. Every one of them is in pursuit of happiness.

To genuinely wish that they all attain exactly what they desire and that their joy always increase until they attain enlightenment—this is the practice of bodhichitta.

BEARING THE UNBEARABLE

In both Western and Tibetan cultures, having a big heart is associated with generosity, kindness, warmth, and compassion. In Tibetan culture, a person with a big heart is also someone with the ability and courage to hold even the most painful truths in his or her heart without becoming despondent.

During difficult times my mother used to say, "You need to make your heart big enough to hold a horse race inside." Working with difficulties in a compassionate way doesn't necessarily mean we can resolve them. Samsara, by its nature, can't be fixed. It can only be worked with and transcended—which means *seen through.*

A traditional Buddhist image of compassion is that of an armless woman watching her only child being swept away by the raging torrent of a river. Imagine the unbearable anguish at not being able to save your child—and not being able to turn away! In the practice of bodhichitta, this is the unconditional compassion we try to cultivate toward all sentient beings, even if we're unable to truly help them until we ourselves become free.

The willingness to not turn away from our anguish as we reflect on the suffering of samsara is the bodhisattva path. This path is possible only because we have seen that the true nature of suffering is egoless, or empty. Not turning away from suffering doesn't mean "toughing it out." It means that, having seen the true nature of suffering, we have the courage to encounter suffering joyfully.

16

Having a Sense of Humor

We could all use more humor in our lives. Having a sense of humor doesn't mean laughing and being cheerful all the time. It means seeing the illusory nature of things—and seeing how, in this illusory life, we are always bumping into the very things we meticulously try to avoid.

Humor allows us to see that ultimately things don't make sense. The only thing that truly makes sense is letting go of anything we continue to hold on to. Our ego-mind and emotions are a dramatic illusion. Of course, we all feel that they're real: my drama, your drama, our confrontations. We create these elaborate scenarios and then react to them. But there is nothing really happening outside of our mind! This is karma's cosmic joke. You can laugh about the irony of this, or you can stick with your scenario. It's your choice.

We need to bring a sense of humor to all aspects of our lives—even to positive aspects such as well-being, harmony, and peace. When we take these things too seriously, joy becomes pain, peace becomes annoying, and harmony becomes contrived. To have genuine harmony, peace, and joy, we need to cut through seriousness with a sense of humor.

Humor can't be described in words. It arises in our heart and a smile appears or laughter comes out of our mouth. It brings a new vision and perspective to everything. And it can also be a great friend—at times our only friend. In especially difficult times, when we're deserted by everyone else, we still have our sense of humor. We don't have to take this short life— with its fathers, mothers, husbands, wives, lovers, children, jobs, and money—so seriously. In fact, it's funny to be so serious. Especially knowing that ultimately we will have to drop all of it and leave this life, as in the Tibetan saying, "like a hair pulled from butter." The brief time that we have in this world would be well spent trying to wake up from seriousness.

IS SERIOUSNESS ALL THAT USEFUL?

There is a lot we could accomplish in this brief human life. We could actually realize the nature of reality and the truth of phenomena—including ourselves. How ridiculous is it then to be so serious about carrying a briefcase, driving a BMW, or talking on the cell phone to our friends? At some point, we have to say, "OK, that's enough." This doesn't mean ignoring our mind and emotions, or not addressing or discussing things. It means simply asking ourselves whether seriousness is all that useful.

Seriousness can be a curse. Before we even get out of bed in the morning, we start planning our day—because if we don't plan ahead, we might just lie there and get nothing done. Then our boss would fire us, our spouse would think we're a terrible person, everyone would think we're a terrible practitioner— and we might agree! Obviously, we must do some planning. But when we take it too seriously, we just torment our mind and body and waste one whole precious day in stress, pain, and confusion.

When we wake up in the morning, thoughts and feelings naturally arise. It's up to us how seriously we take them. Some people don't take things very seriously at all; they may even seem a bit spaced out. But these people get through the day with less stress on the mind and body than people who take things so seriously. This is not to say we should never be serious or responsible. It just means that we may need some perspective and a more positive attitude.

A positive attitude doesn't mean just thinking good thoughts. It means not getting caught up in the seriousness of everything we do, hear, see, feel, and relate with. I myself am very tired of being so serious—exhausted, actually. But it doesn't help to just give up on the things we're so serious about. That doesn't really serve the purpose. What helps is having more lightness and humor.

When you find yourself stuck in seriousness—even if it's your karma to be a very serious person—you can just pop out of it. This is quite a profound practice.

THE SENSE OF HUMOR PRACTICE

Like an old man watching children at play, we need to see through our own seriousness. No matter how seriously the children go about their games, the old man is amused and never for a moment takes them to be real. We can watch our thoughts and emotions in the same way. Without taking them so seriously, we can see them as children at play and give them lots of space. This is how the mind of a practitioner should be.

It is never too early—or too late—to start a "sense of humor practice." In the *Treasury of Dharmadhatu*, Künkhyen Longchenpa describes the experience of all his ordinary reference points falling by the wayside. In essence, he says:

> Since I have come to this realization, all my reference points have fallen away. The ground for clinging to an "'I" and "you" has now collapsed. Where is "you" and where am "I" myself? Who is friend and who is foe? In this wild, chaotic state, everything spontaneously arises

in its own good time and in its own good way. When I look at others, they seem like children—taking things to be real that are not real, taking things to be true that are not true, trying to possess the unpossessable. Ha, ha! I burst out laughing at this amazing spectacle.*

At this stage of realization, we can see the magical nature of appearances as they arise. Trying to nail them down as right or wrong, good or bad, accurate or inaccurate would seem to be a humorous and curious thing to do indeed.

The key to a better sense of humor and more positive attitude is self-reflection. This brings an appreciation of impermanence. Seeing that nothing is solid or permanent, you begin to make yourself at home in the unknown. Then you can experience the lightness and freshness of things as they truly are. It is possible to actually live your life this way.

The bottom line is this: Don't take yourself and your emotions too seriously. Find another "self" to identify with. This doesn't mean creating a split personality; it means identifying with your true nature. Then you won't take ego's emotions so seriously. Even as you go about doing habitual things, if you have a sense of humor about it, ego won't rule your life. The most important heart connection you can have with yourself—just you and yourself—is a heartfelt sense of humor.

TREATING EGO AS A CLOWN

Imagine treating ego as a clown. Clowns are intriguing. They can make us laugh, but they can also become mean or even vicious. You need to be careful around clowns, because they could

---

* Paraphrased and translated from the Tibetan text *Chos dbyings rinpoche'i mdzod*, also known as the *Chöying Dzö*, by Longchenpa.

get you in trouble by making fun of you or making a scene at your expense. You might even want to sit at the back of the room and get ready to defend yourself if they get too aggressive. The point is, you have to be awake around clowns. In just the same way, you have to be on alert when it comes to ego. Otherwise ego's antics may throw you for a loop!

Once when I was talking about seeing ego as a clown, a man in the audience got very upset. Later I learned he was a professional clown, and he was very unhappy to hear clowns used as an example for ego. Since ego is generally vilified in Buddhist teachings, he felt I was putting down clowns—which shows that even clowns are tormented by taking ego so seriously. Later he took part in a bodhisattva vow ceremony. When he came up for his name, taken from a stack of names I'd written earlier that day, coincidentally it turned out to be "King of Laughter." After that, he was quite OK.

Sometimes when we're upset, depressed, or having physical difficulties, it's hard to have a sense of humor about anything, let alone ego. But not taking things too seriously is a good start. When the seriousness becomes too much, just say, "OK, that's enough!" And do something to shake it off: jump up and down, roll in the sand, dive into cold water to wake yourself up—just don't dive in with your eyeglasses on. But whatever you do, don't stay stuck. The more effort you put into letting go, the sooner you will see it really works.

As Shantideva said, "There is nothing that doesn't get easier with practice." When you can really laugh from your heart and your gut, everything opens up. Then you won't be like a professional clown: funny for others, but very serious about yourself.

Young girls are very fortunate because they giggle a lot. True giggles, not nervous or self-conscious giggles, are a kind of massage for the heart. They help us touch the joy in our lives.

Giggles, laughter, and the kind of "ha, ha, ha" that old men make when they laugh with their bellies shaking—they all help us to not take this short life too seriously.

Not Expecting Samsara to Get Any Better

No matter how bad things seem, how could we expect them to be any better? Everything is part of the wheel of samsara. We can't escape from birth, old age, sickness, and death. And we can't just stare in the mirror squeezing our pimples or feeling awful about getting old. We *can* have a sense of humor about these stages of life.

When the time comes to be sick, we don't have to be grumpy or angry with ourselves and others. With a sense of humor, we can be pleasantly sick. And when the time comes to die, we can die with a real sense of humor and joy about our life because we have met the Three Jewels, become a practitioner, and glimpsed the nature of mind. We have seen the illusory quality of thoughts and emotions—and we know that taking them too seriously would defeat the purpose of everything we're trying to do.

Liberation is found wherever discursive thoughts truly dissolve. Whether they spin to the left or the right or around in circles, thoughts are just thoughts. They are dissolved through practice and a sense of humor. To get beyond them would be wonderful, but if you can't, it's wonderful just to have that inspiration. Discursive thoughts and emotions *themselves* are wonderful if we have a sense of humor. We can enjoy them the way an old man enjoys watching children at play. Then thoughts become what they truly are instead of something they're not.

This is what we want from practice. At every stage of the

Buddhist path, we are in search of the truth. We can get to the truth of what is by letting things be. As is said, meditation is much better when it is not fabricated; lake water is much clearer when you don't stir it up—which means *let it be.*

Part Three

FINDING OUR PLACE
IN THE WORLD

17

Action and Intention

Most of us spend a great deal of time trying to find our place in the world. We may not consciously think, "What will I become? What is the meaning of my life? Where do I belong?" But at some subtle level of our mind, we struggle to find our place. No one wants to be born merely to grow up, live an average life, and then die. We all want to find meaning in our lives. We want to fulfill some sense of purpose—we just don't know what it is. And if we don't know what our true purpose is, how can our actions bear out our intention?

Meanwhile, it is very demanding just to stay alive. We may truly struggle doing whatever we need to do to survive. If survival were our only interest, however, we could look to any animal for inspiration; animals do this quite well. But this won't help us find our true meaning or purpose, nor will the many rules and regulations for fitting into society. When we're preoccupied with these conventions, it never occurs to us to look beyond our nose for our life's purpose.

Of course, from ego's perspective, the struggle to survive and find a successful place in society is our purpose. It just doesn't bring any lasting happiness or satisfaction. This is because ego's agendas—such as the attainment of power, wealth, and fame—all depend on specific contexts for their very existence.

Fame, for example, depends on the context of an adoring audience. But people's whims and fancies change constantly from place to place, culture to culture, group to group, person to person. In one context we're a star and put on a pedestal; in another, our talent and status mean nothing. So trying to sustain our famous identity brings no freedom or lasting satisfaction.

Ego's basic agenda is to maintain an identity—but how can we maintain anything in a world that is ever changing and complex? Even our thoughts and emotions are constantly changing. With such shifty reference points, our composure is easily shaken and we can quickly lose heart.

When we feel shaken inside, we don't know what to do or where we belong in the world. Everything we encounter seems threatening. This pandemonium is created by ego. What better way to find out who we really are than by turning away from all this chaos and complexity!

SIMPLIFYING OUR LIFE

The path of Dharma leads us away from ego's struggle to confirm an "identity" and points us toward the bigger vision of benefiting others. Even a momentary thought of benefiting others cuts through the mayhem of ego. It does this by reducing self-importance. This is our deepest intention on the path of Dharma. With less self-importance, life becomes very straightforward and simple.

Simplifying our life doesn't just mean cleaning out the closets and taking things to the Salvation Army. It means having a clear intention or purpose, then supporting that purpose with the way we live our life and direct our mind. In some sense, this is still a context, but it is not a context based on ego and ego's unreliable world. The longing to reduce self-importance and benefit beings is the context of Dharma. Living our life within this context brings our actions together with our deepest intention—which simplifies life incredibly.

Working within the context of Dharma is challenging. Because we are used to identifying with ego, we're hit hard by the pain of ego's defeats. In time, however, the defeat of self-importance brings us satisfaction and relief. We begin to feel more resilient as we rise above ego, instead of "going under." Confusion and chaos settle down and we begin to relax.

People change dramatically when this happens. Those who are hard and stubborn become more open and reasonable; proud people become pleasant to work with; arrogant people give in and surrender. There is no need to fight or hook the world when we no longer feel insecure. There is no need to be something that we are not. Eventually, we can lay claim to our life and find our place in the world.

At this point, we may find nothing more enjoyable than contemplating the Dharma: the preciousness of a human birth, karma, impermanence and death, and the suffering of samsara. We can actually taste the truths of conditioned existence, and we can taste the freedom of the Dharma. This naturally brings compassion for others and their struggles in samsara. We wish for all those who are unaware of the cause of suffering to be free from suffering. When we hold this wish deeply within us, the aspiration of bodhichitta is born.

SOLITUDE

When we focus on benefiting others, something changes in our attitude and approach to life. We feel a greater longing to expose self-importance. We want to look more deeply and move closer to the truth. Our practice becomes more important than running around pretending to be somebody—even a bodhisattva. This longing is often expressed as a desire to be alone.

Socializing with friends and family and getting excited about things we used to get excited about no longer attract us.

We want to spend more time alone, observing our mind closely and seeing how far we've come. This becomes our priority and our path to freedom and peace.

There are times for going out into society and relating with the world, and there are times for going deeper into your practice and gaining more confidence in the teachings. At such times, you need to find some quiet place for practice and not get lost in distractions.

The solitude of nature brings a touch of melancholy or sadness to the mind. Alone with the trees and wind and the birds, ants, and wild animals, you naturally begin to reflect more deeply. As your view of what is meaningful becomes more vast, your sense of melancholy deepens. You may notice something ironic: sitting quietly alone, you may feel less isolated from the world than you do when you're busily engaged in the hustle and bustle of your everyday lives.

Some people feel a strong attraction to this unfamiliar feeling of melancholy—and others, a strong urge to run away. In either case, the important thing is to appreciate our underlying sadness. It is a hint of a deeper intelligence that is normally obscured by the distractions of daily life. In solitude, this natural faculty of our mind comes out of an almost dormant state. Looking out at the natural beauty around us, we realize how much there is to appreciate beyond the narrow focus of ego—and how meaningless is our madly driven life.

The many distractions that we usually find so significant become less important or pointless. We see how, instead of entertaining us, they generate the hassles of gathering and maintaining, and how this endless cycle of busyness ties up our intelligence. In solitary retreat, we can put our intelligence to better use: We can use it to achieve something of true and lasting benefit for this life.

Spending time in solitude allows many positive qualities to break through the crust of mundane mind—and all of them point to the source of true happiness and freedom from suffering. This is our natural birthright. As our confidence gradually deepens, the Dharma becomes a joy; like a radiant light, it illuminates ego-mind and this confused world. What better refuge could we find than this?

TRUE IDENTITY, TRUE FOCUS

The purpose of life is to attend to the self—not the ego "self" but the true nature of all sentient beings. Recognizing this, we find our true purpose and place in the world.

From our true identity arises the true focus of our life: the aspiration to benefit others. Context doesn't matter here, because we are true to ourselves wherever we are. We are not searching for anything, and so we feel at home anywhere. We're not looking for companions, so we can enjoy the companionship of our mind, the lineage, and the Three Jewels. And we don't need a "special" relationship, because we feel a kinship with all beings. We have found the true focus for a meaningful life, which is the welfare of all living beings.

By expanding our mind beyond the confines of ego, we find our place in the world. In this way, we bring our actions together with our deepest intention.

18

Awake in Daytime, Sleep, and Dreams

Genuine meditation is about observing the mind. This is our practice and path. By observing the mind in waking life, sleep, and dreams, we can learn the answers to so many questions.

Why, for example, do most of us wake up feeling groggy and somewhat exhausted? Even though the day is fresh and newly born, we rarely wake up with a fresh, clear state of mind. This is because in our dream state we are continuously caught up in the momentum of conceptual mind.

In order to wake up with a sense of "first moment," we need to change the way we live in the world and relate to our mind. When we don't get caught up in the momentum of delusion, we can be present in our waking and sleeping life—and we won't wake up feeling so stale.

Given the fact that the universe is in a state of constant flux, why do things seem so "old" most of the time? So old that we feel a sense of nausea toward the years, months, weeks, and days; toward ourselves and others and the things that we do, eat, and wear? This feeling of ennui comes from not seeing the freshness of every moment. It comes when we forget that yesterday is now gone, today is a new day, and every moment is changing. When we stop seeing the freshness of each moment, our attitude becomes stale.

Attitude has to do with the way we carry ourselves. It's the way our heart opens or closes when a sense of sweetness, sourness, happiness, or depression arises in our mind. We have many habitual attitudes we may not even be aware of. Habitual attitudes give way to mental gossip and all kinds of emotional conflicts. Mental gossip just floats on the surface. Stopping it can be as easy as picking up a book and starting to read. But the underlying attitude or emotional tenor often remains, unnoticed.

For instance, I've observed many students entering the sangha with a strong attitude of specialness. They may engage in community activities, but this underlying attitude of specialness colors the way they relate to others, the teachings, and their own practice. They often find themselves isolated and in conflict with others. It takes some time relating to the sangha for this to wear away. Once a student clearly sees the source of this attitude, he or she develops genuine appreciation for the unique opportunity the sangha provides.

Stale attitudes are the subtle programming of the mind. They preclude any sense of freshness or appreciation by putting everything into mental "files." You don't really have to look at something and take it in; you think you already know what it is, how it works, and what it means. You may not even notice that you've lost your sense of curiosity and are taking your life for granted.

A DIFFERENT KIND OF DAY
Seeing the newborn quality of life has nothing to do with our experiences being positive or negative. Not every experience is like a nice cup of English tea—but we could look forward to it anyway. Fighters entering the ring are not looking forward to

pleasant experiences; they're looking for a fight. In the same way, we can look forward to whatever our karma presents. This outlook dissolves the stale attitudes and habitual programming of mind.

Much of this programming—with all of its information and survival skills—is based on fear. We're sent to kindergarten, school, college, or vocational school to learn to survive in the mainstream culture. As we learn survival skills, we develop definitive conclusions about the world and how to move about in it. In this way, ego-mind becomes programmed to support our survival.

To free ourselves from this programming, we must experience the unchanging, true nature of mind. Mind's basic nature has a clear, discerning intelligence that is open, inquisitive, and free of fixation. Because it's not stuck in programmed preconceptions, this intelligence has the agility to adapt to any and all change. It is the open, inquisitive mind we had as a child.

Inquisitiveness provides the spark of fundamental truth in our experience. As we begin to encounter life as it is, instead of the way we habitually see it, we come to recognize its original nature. Then waking up in the morning becomes a very different experience. We wake up to a day that unfolds by itself. Because we don't rush to any conclusions about our new day, we have more room to relax.

This doesn't mean we can't function in the world because we're so busy observing impermanence or strengthening our practice of mindfulness. It means that mindfulness is all-pervasive. Whether we're working, cooking, walking, or socializing, we bring an open, fresh attitude to everything we do. And this brings us what we have wanted all along—a different kind of day.

THE STUFF OF DREAMS

Generally, sleep marks the end of our day; we "call it a day" and go to sleep. Otherwise we would just keep going because—other than the fact that we have to sleep—we don't really have a relationship with sleep. It's almost an imposition on our life. And it is often fraught with anxieties: Will I be able to sleep, or will I spend the night tossing and turning, reading the paper, and switching the light on and off? Just approaching the bedroom can be anxiety-provoking.

Our sleep would be different if we could transform our day, because sleep is a continuation of the day. In the daytime, we experience a constantly changing outer world with its rising and setting sun, light, colors, and scenery. Although we can't escape the sensory stimulation of our daytime mind, we *do* expect it to switch off at night. But mind is still awake as we sleep.

When we first fall asleep, our daytime experiences disappear. We hit the bottom of our alaya, or unconscious state of nonthought, with a "gong!" This is a very important natural process. After the barrage of our waking experiences, even great experiences, this blackout in the alaya is a satisfying change. It rejuvenates us. All the energy that drained away through sensory stimulation is restored.

We've all experienced this. A deep nap during the day—for a few seconds, five minutes at the most—can be more powerful than a whole night's sleep. Hitting the bottom of our alaya quickly restores our physical and mental energy. But after some time, we begin to dream—and then we're in another world.

Human beings don't need telescopes to discover other worlds. The world of dreams operates according to a completely different set of rules than our daytime world. It is different outwardly in terms of our sense perceptions and inwardly in terms of how mind relates to them.

In dream states, we may or may not be present in our usual form; we may be flying, or we may be dead. We're not hindered by the physical laws of nature, such as gravity. We can do all sorts of things we can't do in waking life or wouldn't have the courage to try—and we can observe ourselves in all these situations.

AWAKE OR ASLEEP

Dreams are spontaneous and full of "special effects." We can appreciate these dream experiences, or we can relate to them with the habitual attitudes that we bring to our daytime experiences. We may worry about a dream being inauspicious, or get attached to a dream that seems favorable. If we fixate on our dream experiences, which we know to be illusory, what does this say about our relationship to our waking experiences?

On the other hand, if we relax and appreciate our dreams without bias, they can be entertaining. We don't need to go to the movies; we just need to go to sleep.

Whether we are awake or asleep, the essential nature of mind remains the same. From this point of view, there is no difference between the dreams we have when we're asleep and the dream of everyday life. Both arise from the same source, which is empty awareness itself. It's like having two pairs of shoes, daytime and dreamtime shoes: We appreciate both of them equally.

From this common ground of awareness arises the freshness of "first moment." We experience this freshness when we free ourselves from the solidity and hard edges of conceptual mind. Then our world begins to soften, and we can move through our lives with grace and elegance.

19

Grace and Elegance

There is nothing more awkward or crude than a person absorbed in self-importance. And there is nothing more graceful and elegant than someone who is not.

Having natural grace and elegance is not about being a "refined" person in the ordinary sense of cultivating beauty, intelligence, and decorum. Nor is it about holding on to youth, wealth, and social status. That type of refinement is based on self-importance—and therefore attachment. It reflects the conventional values of society and requires us to constantly adjust our self-image for worldly effect. But it never resolves our inner conflicts, awkwardness, and insecurity.

Natural grace and elegance come from inner resolve. We find inner resolve when we let go of attachments in the face of life's challenges.

AGING GRACEFULLY

The greatest challenges we face in the course of human life are aging, sickness, and death. At some point, we must let go of this body. No matter how hard we try, we can't hold on to our body's youthfulness, comfort, fitness, and abilities. If we're attached to these things, we will be in conflict with the natural events of old age, sickness, and death. And we will waste all of our time, energy, and money struggling to hold on to youth. Now, there is nothing wrong with cosmetics, vitamins, exercise, and so on—unless we're using them to hold on. When our ego-mind is struggling to hold on, there is no elegance and grace in our life.

It's difficult enough to age gracefully in such speedy times. With the degeneration of our cultures, traditions, and environment, and with our constantly shifting emotional world, do we even stand a chance? How can we find the time or space in our lives for elegance and grace?

It used to be that old age was a time of relaxation. With age came the space to be ordinary and authentic. This kind of ordinariness is very profound. This is where natural elegance and grace actually come from. But in our fast-paced modern world, we don't see many older people relaxing in public places. They're shoved into nursing homes and kept busy with television, exercise, and other programs. In Europe or New York City, you might still see an old man or woman sitting in a chair, gazing out at the world with a sparkle in their eyes—but it's rare.

We are living at a much faster pace and going through much faster changes than our parents did. Aging is going to be harder for us. We really don't have the time to get old or the space for elegance and grace. Thinking about this, we can appreciate what it means to have the Dharma in our lives. Through practice and self-reflection, we can cultivate our inner strength and well-being.

THE PRACTICE OF LETTING GO

We all have attachments that need to be let go of: outer attachments, inner philosophical and psychological attachments, and some very basic hang-ups, such as trying to avoid death and hold on to youth. You may think you don't have any such attachments—but when the right circumstances arise, you will fall prey to them like anyone else.

Until we let go of attachments, we really only care about what happens to *us*. If *we* win the lottery, we get excited; if someone else wins, we don't. When attachments are let go of, we don't really care who wins the lottery. We're happy that such a thing could happen in this world. We enjoy the achievements and pleasures of others as much as we enjoy the sun, moon, sky, and clouds. Nobody owns them, and there is no sense of "Why isn't that mine?" Because we're not attached to any of it, the world and everything in it is like a beautiful adornment of our presence of mind.

Imagine a king who never resolves the conflicts of being a monarch: the seductions, responsibilities, worries, and pain. He might become rigid, solid, and completely unable to enjoy his kingdom, with its beautiful natural resources and human achievements. But what if there were a beggar or minstrel in the kingdom whose mind was resolved? Then he or she would be the one to manifest presence of mind and to move about the kingdom enjoying all its richness. So no matter who we are or what we possess, the only thing that really matters is letting go of attachment and making room for presence of mind.

In order to let go, the most important thing to understand is that our attachments are nothing other than empty awareness. If you regard them as ornaments adorning the space of your mind, it is easier to let them arise and let them go. Recognizing that everything arises from the same insubstantial awareness, just let whatever arises return to its source. In this way, attachments and conflicts will resolve themselves. This is the most profound way to work with attachment and resolve the mind.

This practice is very ordinary and no big deal. We're not practicing to feel good or to justify our lives, or to be different from or above anyone else. We're not practicing to command respect, to be the one "in the know," or to tell people how to live their lives. We are practicing to let go of inner conflict, or attachment: inner attachments, outer attachments, and attachment to "self" altogether.

Letting go brings a sense of ordinariness that is very profound. When we look at great teachers such as Dilgo Khyentse Rinpoche or His Holiness the Dalai Lama, we see tremendous grace and elegance shining out from their presence. There is no clumsiness of body, speech, and mind, because there is no self-importance or attachment to some self-image. Such a person might accidentally spill tea while pouring it into a cup. But there is no clumsiness in their world, because there is no clumsiness in their mind.

We, on the other hand, would feel tremendously clumsy if we spilled tea. If we weren't so attached to how things should be, our inner struggle wouldn't manifest as awkwardness and embarrassment—and our tea pouring would always be elegant and gracious, even if we spilled.

Some teachers sleep much of the time. But they are not sleeping because they are depressed. Their sleeping is an expression of their elegance and grace. There is no sense of "This is practice and that is not." The line between practice and non-practice has become totally transparent. Their elegance and grace reflect presence of mind in everything they do.

PRESENCE OF MIND

A mind that is resolved is simply present. We are not struggling with good or bad, right or wrong, life or death. We're not trying to reshape our mind through Dharma practice or anything else. We have the presence of mind to simply enjoy our life—good or bad, right or wrong, "dharmic" or not. We take great pleasure in the world and the people around us, and we walk in the world with elegance and grace.

The ability to let go of attachment and resolve our mind is the result of practice and understanding. This achievement is somewhat beyond ordinary human experience; it is extraordinary. But we are not walking alone on this path. Countless beings have gone before us, and countless others are yet to come. To think that we're special would defeat the whole purpose of the path.

With presence of mind, we experience a sense of relaxation and inner resolve in the face of life's challenges. The natural grace and elegance of inner resolve are a measure of a practitioner's life.

20

Creativity

You may think that, having established a meditation practice in your life, you will always be happy and everything will go smoothly. It could happen—it's possible. But most of us will encounter difficulties on the path of Dharma. The biographies of the great masters tell us that they all went through difficulties, challenges, and disappointments. They used these challenges to deepen their practice, and it pushed them to discover a treasury of hidden inner resources.

Like these masters before us, we need not become discouraged when we experience difficulties. Otherwise we might lose our trust and faith in the Three Jewels; we might even lose heart and give up on going deeper into practice altogether.

Most of us enter the path of practice because we can see the unreliability of samsara. We can see that instead of the lasting happiness and well-being we all hope for, samsara produces pain. The teachings resonate with us because they speak directly to this question of happiness and pain—and we long to go deeper. We long to cultivate the causes of happiness: bodhichitta motivation and devotion to the teacher and the Three Jewels.

But what do you do when the emotions you long for don't arise? When instead of devotion, you feel disconnected; instead of compassion, you feel bogged down in self-absorption; and instead of feeling "awake," you feel flat and uninspired? What happens when instead of feeling appreciated, you feel ignored, and instead of feeling at peace, you feel immensely agitated most of the time?

At times like these, you may conclude that you're doing something wrong—or that the Dharma doesn't work. If you take this thought further, you might become suspicious of others on the path and decide it's all a big, deluded hoax. And you certainly won't see the possibility of transcending these limitations. But most of these problems can be overcome by simply being more creative about integrating the Dharma into your life.

USING OUR INNER RESOURCES

Being creative means finding personal ways to engage the wisdom of the Dharma and bring it to life. This means relying on our intelligence rather than expecting the Dharma to change us.

When we face difficulties, it forces us to uncover inner resources we never knew we had. In less affluent societies, people tend to their basic needs through their own resourcefulness. If something is broken, they need to figure out how to fix it. There is not necessarily a manual for everything. In the village in India where I grew up, you see this all the time. For example, someone will make a prayer wheel out of a plastic jar. If something electrical is broken, they will experiment and somehow resolve the problem. This might be a bit dangerous at times, but it forces people to use their inner intelligence and creativity. There is no other choice. When it comes to integrating the Dharma into our life in a personal way, it is the same.

Of course, we must first understand the basic principles of Dharma. But how we integrate them and make them personal is key. When we understand the basic principles of Dharma, we can be creative instead of predictable in relating to people and circumstances. In any situation, we have to ask: What works? What would be the most helpful or beneficial way to apply the teachings? Then see what you come up with. Be especially creative about applying the Dharma to difficult circumstances. During the Communist Chinese invasion of Tibet, many practitioners were jailed and even tortured for up to twenty years. Many of them used these difficult situations to deepen and enhance their practice. What could be more creative than this? When you do things differently—and in accord with the Dharma—you will be an inspiration to yourself and others.

I once heard a story from Eastern Tibet. The Chinese soldiers were lining up monks for execution. As he was about to be shot, one monk cried out, "May I take the suffering of all sentient beings upon myself. May I exhaust my own and others' negative karma." Observers reported that he showed no sign of fear and was completely calm when he died.

In the most futile circumstances—even in our last moment—we can access our inner resources. By applying them, we transform our situation. Such is the power of creative mind.

INNATE INTELLIGENCE IS NEVER STUCK

Most of us long for a sense of connection to our spiritual path— and in general, we all want to feel good. When we actually *do* feel deeply connected to practice, we get excited and try to hold on to this feeling, which we associate with being "on track." But feelings are temporary and eventually fade.

On the other hand, when our practice feels flat and uninspiring, we feel stuck with this state of mind. But the very intelligence that knows we're stuck is itself not stuck. Therefore, we have a choice: We can choose to identify with our innate intelligence, or we can choose to identify with temporary thoughts and feelings.

When we identify with our thoughts and feelings, they seem to be valid. And they seem to be valid because they're "mine." When they're rooted in self-importance, even noble thoughts—wishing to feel connected to practice, for example— can get us stuck.

But our innate intelligence is never stuck. When we use our innate intelligence, there is no limit to the ways in which we can creatively respond to whatever confronts us. This is the way we make the Dharma personal.

For example, the next time you feel disconnected from the practice, rouse your bodhichitta. This brings you out of your self-absorption and automatically connects you to others. Or, if your mind is hindered by negative thoughts, try contemplating impermanence and the preciousness of a human birth. Such positive thoughts provide sustenance for the practice. You can also turn to study, particularly on the view of emptiness, which is a powerful way to clear obstacles that hinder our deeper intelligence. Ultimately, if you can let this unwanted feeling of disconnection be, it will exhaust itself.

The important thing to remember is that experiences such as disconnection are not the problem. It's the reaction to them that creates so much pain. As the great Indian mahasiddha Tilopa said to his disciple Naropa: "Son, it is not appearances that bind you, but your reactions* to them. Therefore, cut your reactions, Naropa!"

TICKET TO REALIZATION
Because they direct us toward understanding our mind in a deeper way, the difficulties, challenges, and disappointments that we all face on our spiritual path can become our ticket to realization.

---

* Tib. *zhen pa*. This term is generally translated as "attachment." However, it refers not only to attachment but also to the more active aspect of clinging found in aversion, pride, jealousy, and so on, and so it is translated here as "reaction."

Without challenges, we would miss the opportunity to know the many aspects of mind that can develop understanding and depth of character. And it is only through intimately coming to know them that we can empathize with the suffering and joy of others. Unless we demystify all the aspects of our mind that intimidate us through self-reflection, we will always assume that they bind us. We will never experience their illusory and magical qualities. Without them we would never be forced to probe more deeply into our innate intelligence—our treasury of innate resources.

If we appreciate our challenges, the practice is always accessible to us. Even when we feel disconnected, we will always remain connected to our spiritual path. Whatever arises can be utilized and appreciated—like a prayer wheel made from a plastic jar.

BREATHING LIFE INTO OUR PRACTICE

The Dharma provides us with the tools to be creative. But working creatively with our practice takes time and effort. It takes time to sit patiently with our ego-mind. And the idea of applying effort to anything spiritual is not a popular notion; we would rather things happen naturally. We would like to think that if we just practice consistently, all of our struggles and confusion will take care of themselves. But how can anything change if we don't fully open and engage our mind?

Unless we are open and awake, the blessings of practice cannot touch us and nothing will change. When our mind is open and engaged, we can integrate the Dharma into our life in vastly creative ways. This breathes life into our practice.

21

Great Possibilities

What makes mind and the phenomenal world so interesting is that neither one of them is fixed. Because they are interdependent—and therefore empty—both mind and the world are flexible and the creative possibilities are great. The key to this realization is emptiness. When we understand that nothing is intrinsically solid or static, our experiences of life and death won't seem so threatening. They might seem more like an amusement park ride.

This is a pointing-out instruction. It points out that ignorance is our only hindrance. Ignorance causes us to see things as solid, static, and absolute, when they're not. Nevertheless, we think we have no choice but to endure the ripening of our karmic seeds and the spawning of their worlds. We forget that mind's seeds and tendencies can be purified by the Dharma.

When ignorance is overcome by the Dharma, we are no longer bound by habitual tendencies, and no further karma is produced. Our mind can expand and let the world in: The world becomes part of mind and mind becomes part of the phenomenal world—and we come very close to experiencing the universe and mind as one.

Experiencing mind and the world in their fullness, we realize their great power and limitless potential for enlightened activity. If this potential can manifest anything and everything on the level of samsara, how much more can it manifest on the level of enlightened activity? It is within our reach to understand and realize this great possibility.

MAGIC, POWER, AND BLESSINGS

Enlightened power does not necessarily arise in the form of magnificent miraculous displays. Even if it did, what good would it do if it had no effect on the suffering of ego-mind? The world is already magical. In a completely blue sky suddenly clouds churn up and there is thunder, lightning, and, from complete emptiness, rain. But we don't think of this as magic; we think of it as ordinary weather. And if an enlightened being performs some magical feat but ego-mind isn't open to it, it will have no more effect on us than the weather.

The blessings of the buddhas and bodhisattvas can only be experienced with the wearing away of self-absorption. When the inherent potential of our mind is engaged, the power of these blessings can transform our mind and circumstances. Things can go from being completely "not OK" one minute to being wholesome and nurturing the next. And seemingly disastrous situations can actually further our understanding of our mind and true nature.

With faith and trust, we can see that the enlightened mind of the buddhas of the ten directions holds the whole universe. It can penetrate anything in creation. And through a limitless variety of skillful means, it makes unceasing efforts for the benefit of sentient beings. Because it is free of the limitations of ignorance, it acts effortlessly: An aeon could become a split second and a split second an aeon. When we open our mind—with all its seeds of incomprehension—we can surrender and trust in this bigger view.

When our experience of the world is this big, it no longer matters what others think or say about us. We know exactly what our place is in this world. Even alone in a cave eating our nettle soup, we feel completely connected to the bigness and richness of the world and all the beings in it—and all the worlds beyond it. We feel as connected to the past and future as we do to the present. Seeing the connectedness of everything opens life up and brings tremendous well-being to the phenomenal world. But this requires trust and faith.

At all levels of practice, it is very important to have faith and trust in yourself. You are so fortunate to have been introduced to the Three Jewels, the buddhas, bodhisattvas, and great beings. How many beings have even heard the name Buddha Shakyamuni? Not many. How many know of Mañjushri, Avalokiteshvara, Vajrapani, Guru Rinpoche, or Tara?* It takes aeons of merit just to hear their names, let alone come to know and have a connection to even one of them. Nothing could be sadder than to have this good fortune and not appreciate or have faith in it. So please take advantage of this opportunity. It will bring you tremendous benefit.

RECLAIMING A LEGACY

The fruition of the path of Dharma is finally realizing our great possibilities. This is like being a prince or princess who, after

---

* Buddha Shakyamuni was the historical buddha of our times, who was born into the noble Indian clan of the Shakyas. *Shakyamuni* literally means "sage of the Shakyas." Mañjushri is the bodhisattva of wisdom and one of the Eight Great Close Sons of the Buddha. He holds aloft the sword of wisdom that cuts through all ignorance. Avalokiteshvara is the bodhisattva of compassion and another of the Eight Great Close Sons. He became the most popular deity of Tibet, under whose realm of protection the Tibetan region falls. Vajrapani is the embodiment of enlightened power or ability, a bodhisattva most often depicted in a wrathful form signifying the direct, uncompromising aspect of enlightened compassion. Guru Rinpoche, also known as Padmasambhava, is the great master who brought the profound teachings of all the yanas of Buddhism to Tibet in the ninth century; he was thus the single most important figure in all of Tibetan Buddhism. Tara is the embodiment of the female aspect of compassion, also referred to as the mother of all the buddhas. She is a bodhisattva known for her quick response to those who call upon her aid.

countless aeons on the road suffering from homelessness, poverty, hunger, thirst, and the abuse of relentless weather, finally discovers his or her kingdom.

You are this prince or princess, in a line of monarchs that has served millions of beings. You can take this precious opportunity to reclaim your kingdom. To do this, you must first realize the strength and qualities of your heritage. Then supplicate for less ignorance and more sharpness and intelligence. By taking possession of the spirit, qualities, and courage of the Buddha's line, you will reach the state of buddhahood. It is not far away. Unlike samsara, it does not need to be created by causes and conditions. It is always present within you.

Please take these words to heart and examine them. The Buddha said, "Examine my words the way a goldsmith examines gold. Don't just take my word because it is my word." Examine everything, not with a sense of obligation or suspicion but with an open mind. If something makes some sense and brings meaning and benefit to your life, apply it creatively. I would be so grateful to have brought something of benefit to your life. This is my only intention.

The last time I spoke with my root teacher, Dilgo Khyentse Rinpoche, he said, "Try to give to others as much of the teachings as possible. Then you might be of some benefit and not waste your life." So please take whatever makes sense to you into your heart. You don't have to understand everything or take it all in—but whatever you do take will truly bring about change in your life.

The potential for realization is universal and present for all of us. True benefit will come from your own efforts and realization. For your efforts to bring benefit, you must take your life into your own hands and examine your mind and experience.

From this point of view, nobody could be kinder to you than yourself. Nobody could have a greater effect on you or actually do more for you than yourself. The Buddha said, "I have shown you the path of liberation. Now liberation depends on you." This is really true. If you don't take your life into your own hands, not even the buddhas can make a difference. It's up to you.

SUGGESTIONS FOR FURTHER READING

Dilgo Khyentse. *Enlightened Courage*. Ithaca, N.Y.: Snow Lion, 1993.

Dilgo Khyentse. *The Heart Treasure of the Enlightened Ones*. Boston: Shambhala Publications, 1992.

Khunu Rinpoche. *Vast as the Heavens, Deep as the Sea: Verses in Praise of Bodhicitta*. Boston: Wisdom Publications, 1999.

Patrül Rinpoche. *The Words of My Perfect Teacher*. Boston: Shambhala Publications, 1998.

Chögyam Trungpa Rinpoche. *Training the Mind and Cultivating Loving-Kindness*. Boston: Shambhala Publications, 1993.

MANGALA SHRI BHUTI
CENTERS

Mangala Shri Bhuti is a nonprofit Tibetan Buddhist organization under the direction of Venerable Dzigar Kongtrül Rinpoche. Mangala Shri Bhuti offers programs on introductory and advanced Buddhist topics by Dzigar Kongtrül Rinpoche and other lineage holders. *It's Up to You* is based on Kongtrül Rinpoche's weekly "personal link" teachings. These teachings can be heard via live streaming audio on the web or by phone. You may also order recordings of Kongtrül Rinpoche's Personal Link teachings and public seminars on standard or mp3 CD. Please visit our Web site for more information. Kongtrül Rinpoche's teaching schedule is also available there.

If you would like more information please contact us.

In Colorado:
Mangala Shri Bhuti
P.O. Box 4088
Boulder, CO 80306
(303) 459-0184

In Vermont:
Pema Ösel Do Ngak Chöling
Study, Contemplation, and Meditation Center
322 Eastman Crossroad
Vershire, VT 05079
(802) 333-4521

On the Internet:
www.mangalashribhuti.org